Legacy of Leaders: A 40-Day Journey with the Men of God's Word

Published by Giving Publishing, 2555 Northwinds Parkway, Alpharetta, GA 30009

In association with WTA Media, Franklin, TN

ISBN: 978-0-5788333-3-0
Written by Robert Noland
Edited by Christy Distler

Legacy
of LEADERS

A 40-Day Journey
with the Men of God's Word

Robert Noland

CONTENTS

In my six-plus decades on the planet and forty-plus years in ministry, the most amazing sight I have ever beheld is a man's heart radically changed by Jesus Christ. And certainly, it is the most incredible thing that has ever happened to me. Especially in our current culture, it is safe to say that a man changing at *all* in any way is a rare event. But when the love and grace of Christ collides with a desperate, broken man, then and only then does true transformation take place.

Such is the story of all the men in *Legacy of Leaders*—an encounter with the living God changed everything.

As transformation occurs and sanctification—the journey of being molded into the image of Jesus—starts, the very next step God offers is the opportunity to become a leader for Him. With the past in the rearview mirror, the future is an invitation to become a part of His legacy.

For our purposes, let's define a leader as someone who goes before the crowd to blaze trails, forge new paths, and discover uncharted territory. But if we call someone a leader, that must also mean someone is following.

Years ago, as I was discussing my calling with a good friend, he told me, "If you think you're a leader but look behind you and no one is following, then guess what? You're not a leader. But if you don't believe you're a leader, yet you look behind you and people are following, then guess what? You're a leader!" So, ultimately, leadership is not so much about the perception of the person out front as it is about the perspective of those following.

Social media has altered the popular definition and connotation of a leader because a celebrity can have millions of "followers," yet not be a leader on any level. In fact, they could be holed up in their mansion with a small entourage who are all on the payroll! Ironic how the culture of these platforms is not about leadership at all, but only about following.

But Jesus can take broken men, in *any* generation, that the world ignores and overlooks and create a leader. Scripture is filled with such stories. Literally from cover to cover in the Bible, we see this same dynamic occur. Whether a man is a murderer and an adulterer or he is upstanding and respected, when God's power lands on his heart, *everything* changes.

That is why I chose to share forty different stories from the Bible with you—to look at the qualities, characteristics, and virtues of how God works in the lives of normal people. I intentionally placed the major focus of each day on the Scripture passage. I "story out" some of the passage for you, but then offer key verses that are crucial to what God did in the man and the event. For years in my live teaching, I have taught exegetically through

Scripture with the goals of letting the Word speak for itself and showing the humanity in each story. The men who God chose were not some race of super-heroes, but broken men just like you and me. Today, like back then, God can work on, in, and through a man to change the world one heart at a time.

Jesus forever redefined the concept of a leader when He stated in three of the Gospels, "Whoever wants to be a leader among you must be your servant. … For even the Son of Man came not to be served but to serve others and to give his life as a ransom for many" (Matthew 20:26–28; Mark 10:43–45, Luke 22:26-27).

Here are a few helpful points I hope will encourage you as you begin your experience:

1. COMMIT

To use this book for the next forty days, setting aside intentional and undistracted time to create a habit of engaging with God daily. If you miss a day or two, just pick back up where you left off. Please don't give in to the temptation to feel any guilt; just jump back in. This is not intended to be a religious exercise but an effort to build a relationship with God. So, don't quit—commit. Your friendship with Christ is worth every moment you invest.

2. DECIDE

The best time in your day that you'll commit to this devotional. Choose a time that will be optimal for your schedule. Weekends may look a bit different from your weekdays.

That's fine. You may need to experiment the first few days, but pick a time and stick with it.

3. **PICK A PLACE**

   Just like Jesus did in Mark 1:35—a quiet and peaceful setting. Choose the most comfortable spot you can find, away from distractions. No phones. No devices. No TV, and no one else around. Your environment is crucial for you to be focused as you engage with God.

4. **READ**

   And take in *all* the content. I worked hard to make every word count, and God certainly did with Scripture. Don't scan, like you do a text or email, but read each day carefully like a personal letter, most importantly the Bible verses. If you prefer to read the Scripture passages provided each day from your own version, feel free to do so. Just look up the day's passage and read your Bible instead. The version is not as crucial as taking in God's Word.

5. **LEADERS' UPWARD AND OUTWARD CONNECTING POINTS**

   are in each of the forty days. There is an *Upward* application question (the vertical icon with a hand pointing up) and also an *Outward* application question (the horizontal icon with a hand pointing to the side). The *Upward* question is about your relationship with God—you and Him. The *Outward* question is about your relationship with others. The purpose of these is to guide you in connecting the day's content to your own life. This pattern follows Jesus' answer to the question of the greatest commandment found in Matthew 22:37–39: "'You must love the Lord your God with all your heart, all your soul, and all your mind.' [Upward] This is the first and greatest commandment. A second is equally important: 'Love your neighbor as yourself. [Outward]'"

The more open and honest you are in your answers, the more opportunity you create for growth in spiritual maturity and leadership development. Taking the time each day to dive deep into this section will help you discover and apply the scriptural and spiritual truths to your own life. If you prefer, you can use your own journal rather than the space provided in the book. Allowing a few minutes to write down your feelings and thoughts is a great way to maximize this experience and process what God is saying to you. When you complete these forty days and go back through what you have written, you will likely be able to see your growth—just like the trek up the mountain on the cover.

6. PRAY

Allowing time each day to speak with God and tell Him everything as you would a best friend (see Exodus 33:11). Just talk to Him. Share what's on your heart and your mind. Be honest. Be specific. No thees and thous or fancy spiritual language is necessary. Simple prayers are provided at the end of each day, if needed. Whether you're learning to pray or deepening in your prayers, these next forty days could revolutionize your life, spiritual growth, and ability to lead.

Be mindful to keep praying as you go through your day and maintain an ongoing dialogue with your Heavenly Father. Remember, He doesn't stay wherever you pray; He goes with you everywhere.

7. **LISTEN AND OBEY**
   after you pray, closing your time with a quiet moment to hear God speak. Be still and know He is God (see Psalm 46:10). Quiet your mind and heart and pray the prayer of Samuel: "Speak, Lord, for your servant is listening" (1 Samuel 3:9). It is normal to feel a little strange at first as you sit and listen, but if you stick with this discipline, you will be amazed at what the Holy Spirit will speak to you. Then obey what you hear and live out what He tells you. That's the ultimate goal of a Christ-follower—to allow Jesus to change your life through a personal relationship with Him.

8. **SCRIPTURE MEMORY VERSES**
   A Bible verse connected to the Scripture focus or topic is offered at the close of each day for you to memorize (see Psalm 119:11). On certain days, I have adapted the verse with blank lines to personalize with your name. God's Word is intended for all, but also to be made intimate from His heart to yours. This approach allows you to place yourself into the application of the verse with the goal of customizing and applying the message of that day to your life.

9. **MOTIVATIONAL ONE-LINERS**
   close out each day. The first is an original leadership quote to

inspire your own work in the world and may also be shared in business and entrepreneurial settings for motivation. If your career is in management of people, these are for you to share. The last one-liner is to inspire and share in any faith setting.

10. USING *LEGACY OF LEADERS* IN A SMALL GROUP

works well. You can agree to go through a day prior to getting together to be ready to discuss what you got from the day or what you wrote down. Your group could also choose to read the day's content aloud in the meeting and spend the bulk of your time talking through the *Upward* and *Outward* connecting points as your discussion questions. This devotional also works well in a leadership-training or discipleship group, because of the over-all theme and strong scriptural focus. Accountability questions are provided at the end of the book. Close by praying for one another.

Jesus called them together and said,
"You know that the rulers in this world
lord it over their **people,**
and officials flaunt their authority
over those under them.
But among **YOU** it will be different.
Whoever wants to be a **leader** among
you must be your servant,
and whoever wants to be **FIRST**
among you must become your slave.
For even the Son of Man
came not to be **served** but to
SERVE OTHERS and to give
HIS LIFE
as a **RANSOM** for many."

MATTHEW 20:25–28

13

NOAH
SURRENDER

GENESIS 6-9

In Genesis 3, we are told of Adam and Eve's choice in the Garden of Eden to disobey God. Just three chapters later, as mankind is populating the earth, we now see the Father surveying the epidemic and systemic state of rebellion. Yet in His character as Creator, God began to unveil a solution, one that also reflected His heart as Redeemer. While He looked at the rest of the world and witnessed only evil, God saw in Noah a deep child-like faith and trust in Him.

Noah was a righteous man, the only blameless person living on earth at the time, and he walked in close fellowship with God. ... Now God saw that the earth had become corrupt and was filled with violence. ... "But I will confirm my covenant with you. So enter the boat—you and your wife and your sons and their wives." ... So Noah did everything exactly as God had commanded him. (Genesis 6:9, 11, 18, 22)

Many historic accounts in the Bible came to a crossroads with a three-letter word that changed everything: *but*. In Genesis 6:8, we find another example: "*But* Noah found favor with the LORD." He was different and separate because of his decision to trust

God at all costs. This one man's life was a reflection of the Father's goodness and loving-kindness, allowing Him to find in Noah the very reason He created people—relationship, fellowship, and partnership with Him.

In verse 9, the words used to describe Noah refer to not only his close relationship with the Lord, but also his impeccable reputation with his neighbors, whether they liked him or not. When no one else would, Noah chose obedience—both in his heart for God and as a witness before his community.

Because we can read the entire Bible today, we must remind ourselves that Noah had no knowledge of the Gospel. No prophecy had yet been given about a coming Messiah. His obedience stemmed simply from his belief that placing faith in the Creator was the right thing to do and the best life to lead.

But as we have seen throughout history, the decision to follow God often comes into direct conflict with those who oppose God and His ways. A lifestyle honoring the Lord in a worldly culture often draws judgment and condemnation. Yet this very dynamic in Noah allowed for God's divine protection and provision for him and his family.

And it is impossible to please God without faith. Anyone who wants to come to him must believe that God exists and that he rewards those who sincerely seek him. It was by faith that Noah built a large boat to save his family from the flood. He obeyed

God, who warned him about things that had never happened be-fore. By his faith Noah condemned the rest of the world, and he received the righteousness that comes by faith. (Hebrews 11:6–7)

God honored those who Noah loved because of his spiritual authority over his household. The Lord declared His covenant was with Noah, his wife, his sons, and their wives as the second generation was chosen to repopulate the earth.

We are inspired throughout Scripture by those who have stood alone, no matter the difficulty of their circumstances, to experience God's amazing favor and blessing by the full surrender of their lives. Because of a relationship with Jesus Christ, you also have the unique opportunity to join these biblical pillars as you choose obedience to God over the culture.

One area of my life that I know God wants me to surrender to Him in faith and obedience is:

_____

_____

_____

_____

_____

_____

_____

The place(s) in my life I have surrendered to God where I am leading now are:

_____

_____

_____

_____

_____

_____

_____

"Heavenly Father, the depth of Noah's faith and surrender to You is hard to fathom. His situation literally came down to just You and him against the world, with his choice of faith being what ultimately saved him and his family. Even though my world is very different, please help me to view my commitment and level of surrender as the same as Noah's. Thank You for salvation through Your grace and the opportunity to lead through constant surrender to You. In Jesus' name, amen."

MEMORY VERSE

AND IT IS IMPOSSIBLE TO PLEASE GOD WITHOUT FAITH.

- HEBREWS 11:6 -

A REPUTATION ABOVE REPROACH
IS BUILT ON A PATH
OF ONE RIGHT DECISION AT A TIME.

Before we can
see God's
CHECKERED
flag of victory
we must first wave
the WHITE FLAG of
surrender.

ABRAHAM
FAITH

GENESIS 15, 22

Throughout history, Abraham's name has always been first in this legendary list: "the God of Abraham, Isaac, and Jacob." His name is included for just one reason: his faith in "the God." Today, we'll look at two integral passages regarding Abram-turned-Abraham.

Some time later, the Lord spoke to Abram in a vision and said to him, "Do not be afraid, Abram, for I will protect you, and your reward will be great." But Abram replied, "O Sovereign Lord, what good are all your blessings when I don't even have a son?" … Then the Lord said to him, "… for you will have a son of your own who will be your heir." Then the Lord took Abram outside and said to him, "Look up into the sky and count the stars if you can. That's how many descendants you will have!" And Abram believed the Lord, and the Lord counted him as righteous because of his faith. (Genesis 15:1–2, 4–6)

This passage, known as "God's Covenant with Abraham," is not someone's fictional conjecture or a romantic tale of fantasy, but an actual conversation placed on record between Maker and man. Picture this scene: God tells a man to look up into the clear night sky and that from him will come more children throughout the generations than the number of stars he can see. Sound crazy? So how did Abraham respond to such a statement? He simply believed in his heart that God's promise was true and that it would be true. Because, of course, he would not live to see the complete outcome.

But there is another event in Scripture that overshadows God's presentation of the promise—the test in Genesis 22. God is true to His word and Abraham had a son, Isaac. No matter how many times you have read or heard the story, this time try to put yourself in Abraham's place.

God told him to take his son up to the mountain and offer him as a sacrifice. Amazingly, Abraham appeared to offer no questioning, no pushback, and no debate. Only obedience. He made the climb, built the altar, tied up his son, and raised the knife. Imagine the horror for both father and son as the question of "Why?" raced through both their minds. But ...

At that moment the angel of the Lord called to him from heaven, "Abraham! Abraham!" "Yes," Abraham replied. "Here I am!" "Don't lay a hand on the boy!" the angel said. "Do not hurt him in any way, for now I know that you truly fear God. You have not withheld from me even your son, your only son." Then Abraham looked up and saw a ram caught by its horns in a thicket. So he took the ram and sacrificed it as a burnt offering in place of his son. (Genesis 22:11–13)

As we read Scripture, we must always keep in mind that these people were normal humans, not superheroes or some heavenly breed given a higher level of faith. Never remove the very raw and real human element as you take in God's Word.

Throughout the many seasons of our lives, God will continually call us to these same two spiritual dynamics, just as He did Abraham:

• Our belief in His calling for our lives
• Our sacrifice to experience His calling in our lives

Deepening in our belief in God will always bring the challenge of sacrifice. To comply, we have to set aside our doubts, struggles, biases, and personal agendas to look at where God is pointing us and respond with, "I believe You, Lord." There are moments when God asks us to "raise the knife" on small, easy, simple things. But there will be those tough times when He calls us to take sacrificial action. We can't yet see the outcome, don't understand what He is doing, or can't envision the reason or purpose for what He is asking. Those are the situations that, just as when God tested Abraham, show us what we truly believe and the true depth of our faith.

God never tests us so He can see what we are made of. He already knows. He tests us so *we* can see what we are made of.

The most difficult test I have experienced in my faith journey has been:

_____

_____

_____

_____

_____

When I chose to sacrifice:

_____

_____

_____

_____

I saw how God began to work and allow me to:

_____

_____

_____

_____

"Heavenly Father, I know that to You, my calling is no less significant than Abraham's. You want my faith and obedience through my own sacrifices to touch my world in Your name for Your glory. Please strengthen my faith to believe and trust You, even in the toughest tests that come into my life. In Jesus' name, amen."

MEMORY VERSE

Write your name in the blank to personalize and memorize this adaptation of today's verse:

AND _____

BELIEVED THE LORD.

- GENESIS 15:6, ADAPTED -

**THE LARGER THE VISION,
THE TOUGHER THE TEST,
THE HARDER THE SACRIFICE,
THE GREATER THE REWARD.**

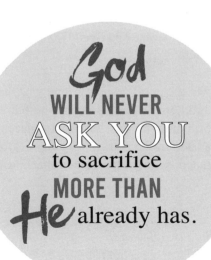

God WILL NEVER ASK YOU to sacrifice MORE THAN *He* already has.

DAY 3

JOSEPH
INTEGRITY

GENESIS 37, 39–41

As we read the life of Joseph in the book of Genesis, a familiar pattern emerges: He was placed in dire circumstances yet chose integrity, and God blessed him. This set a precedent that continued for many years until he came into a position of blessing for himself with the authority to bless a nation.

Integrity has everything to do with a constant adherence to a code of conduct. In Joseph's case and ours, that code is Jesus-focused and Bible-centered.

In Genesis 37, we see that because Joseph was their father's favored son, his brothers' jealousy, anger, and hatred drove them to sell him to Midianite traders for twenty pieces of silver (ten fewer than Judas got for the betrayal of Jesus). After their arrival in Egypt, the traders sold Joseph to Potiphar, Pharaoh's captain of the guard.

From the day Joseph was put in charge of his master's household and property, the LORD began to bless Potiphar's household for Joseph's sake. All his household affairs ran smoothly, and his crops and livestock flourished. (Genesis 39:5)

Consider these questions:

- Did Joseph have a choice in *what* was happening in his life? No.

- Did Joseph have a choice in how he *responded* to what was happening in his life? Yes.

- Could Joseph have decided to live his life as a victim of his brothers' evil? Yes.

- How might Joseph's story have been different had he decided to trade his integrity for bitterness, hatred, and revenge?

But things only get worse. Joseph was falsely accused of coming on to Potiphar's wife and was thrown into prison. But he was totally innocent. Yet again, out of tragedy his amazing attitude of integrity prevailed. And so did God's blessings.

Before long, the warden put Joseph in charge of all the other prisoners and over everything that happened in the prison. The warden had no more worries, because Joseph took care of everything. The Lord was with him and caused everything he did to succeed. (Genesis 39:22–23)

By now, Joseph could have been a whiny, depressed, bitter, class-A jerk. But the *consequences* from his choice of integrity constantly changed his *circumstances* to the best they could be in his *current* situation. No matter the choices of others, Joseph chose the right path. Whatever he did, whether in word or action, he did it for the glory of God (see Colossians 3:17).

After years spent in prison, Joseph was finally summoned to interpret Pharaoh's dreams. He successfully deciphered them and offered advice of what to do to prepare for the predicted coming famine, and the Egyptian leader responded in amazement.

Joseph's suggestions were well received by Pharaoh and his officials. So Pharaoh asked his officials, "Can we find anyone else like this man so obviously filled with the spirit of God?" Then Pharaoh said to Joseph, "Since God has revealed the meaning of the dreams to you, clearly no one else is as intelligent or wise as you are. You will be in charge of my court, and all my people will take orders from you. Only I, sitting on my throne, will have a rank higher than yours." (Genesis 41:37–40)

Is there a relationship, place, or situation in your life where calling upon your highest level of integrity and upping your attitude could change everything to open up the opportunity for God to bless you? Being a man of integrity is not a quality or characteristic, but a choice.

My most difficult circumstance right now where
I need God to help me choose integrity is:

_____

_____

_____

_____

_____

_____

I have experienced God allowing me to bless
others when I chose integrity in this situation:

_____

_____

_____

_____

_____

_____

"Heavenly Father, the pattern of Joseph was amazing, as he kept being thrown into bad situations but constantly maintained his integrity. He always chose You and Your ways over His own. Help me to view the tough obstacles in my life not as roadblocks but rather on-ramps to growth that allow You to move and work in me. In Jesus' name, amen."

MEMORY VERSE

Write your name in the blank to personalize and memorize this adaptation of today's verse:

THE LORD WAS WITH _____

AND CAUSED EVERYTHING HE DID TO SUCCEED.

- GENESIS 39:23, ADAPTED -

ALWAYS CHOOSE THE ATTITUDE OF LIVING IN VICTORY
OVER THE ATROPHY OF LIVING AS A VICTIM.

BEING A
MAN
of
integrity
is not a
quality
or
CHARACTERISTIC,
BUT A
CHOICE.

MOSES
SERVANT-LEADER

EXODUS 32–33

In the highlight montage of Moses' life, the encounter with the burning bush, the manifestation of the plagues upon Pharaoh's Egypt, and the parting of the Red Sea would be obvious featured segments. But there is a conversation with God that depicted the level of sacrificial commitment Moses had for the Lord and the people he led. Here is a recap of the backstory from Exodus, leading up to that encounter.

God had given Moses the plans for the Tabernacle, the Ark, and the role of the priests in great detail. Moses was then given the stone tablets inscribed by God's own finger. Next, the Lord warned Moses that the people had fashioned a golden calf to worship as their "god," led by none other than Moses' right-hand man, Aaron. In Moses' absence, they were partying like heathens at the foot of the mountain. God then said He was going to destroy the people and start over with just Himself and Moses.

Moses pleaded with God to relent. God listened and honored Moses' request. Moses then came back down the mountain, witnessed the people's rebellion for himself, broke the tablets, and started to clean up their mess.

If you were in Moses' place, what actions would have run through your mind? But regardless of what he may have considered or been tempted to do, Moses came to an amazing offer of resolve.

The next day Moses said to the people, "You have committed a terrible sin, but I will go back up to the Lord on the mountain. Perhaps I will be able to obtain forgiveness for your sin." So Moses returned to the Lord and said, "Oh, what a terrible sin these people have committed. They have made gods of gold for themselves. But now, if you will only forgive their sin—but if not, erase my name from the record you have written!" (Exodus 32:30–32)

Moses offered up his own life as a sacrifice to God to atone for the people's sins. When they were busy with sin, he was innocent, standing in the Lord's presence. This is, of course, one of many Old Testament foreshadowings of what Jesus would eventually carry out once and for all for all humanity. But the fact remained that as God's servant-leader to the people, Moses was willing to give up his life to satisfy the Lord and serve the people as their leader.

Maybe you are or have been a first responder, in the military, or in some other form of service where you understand being regularly called upon to literally risk your life for others. Regardless, a man who steps up to be a leader in this world on God's behalf will be asked on a regular basis to sacrifice his own desires, needs, and agenda for the sake of others. There are constant opportunities as well as challenges to put someone else first for the Kingdom of God.

But how did Moses come to such a sacrificial level of servant-leadership? How did he gain such a strong sense of eternal perspective that he would offer his life? The answer can be found in Exodus 33:11.

Inside the Tent of Meeting, the Lord would speak to Moses face to face, as one speaks to a friend.

Serving God and others as Jesus' greatest commandment tells us to do is not a natural response, but supernatural. As sinners, we cannot sustain giving of ourselves in our own strength for very long. Our selfishness fights sacrifice. Our self-preservation battles service. The only way we can offer up our lives as Moses did is found in Exodus 33:11. We see the same dynamic and discipline in Jesus' life. One such example is Mark 1:35: *"Before daybreak the next morning, Jesus got up and went out to an isolated place to pray."*

Navigating life, family, and career while serving anyone in our circles of influence can be a deeply personal tension every day. But spending time face-to-face with God through a relationship with Jesus, talking as a friend talks with a friend, is the key to continuing to be His servant-leaders.

The hardest aspect for me right now, where I need God's help in being a servant-leader is:

_____

_____

_____

_____

_____

_____

The place (or places) where I know God uses me to be His servant-leader are:

_____

_____

_____

_____

_____

_____

"Heavenly Father, thank You that the example of Your being our best Friend and closest Confidant can be seen throughout Scripture from Moses to Jesus. Help me to always keep in mind that the time I spend with You is the only way I can stay equipped and empowered to serve You and those around me in my circles of influence. In Jesus' name, amen."

MEMORY VERSE

Write your name in the blank to personalize and memorize this adaptation of today's verse:

INSIDE THE TENT OF MEETING, THE LORD WOULD SPEAK TO _____ *FACE TO FACE, AS ONE SPEAKS TO A FRIEND.*

- EXODUS 33:11, ADAPTED -

A SERVANT-LEADER LIVES
ON THE FRONT LINES,
NOT IN THE CORNER OFFICE.

Your FACE-TO-FACE TIME with GOD IS THE BEST *investment* you will ever make in your life.

JETHRO
WISE COUNSEL

EXODUS 18

Having Moses for a son-in-law might have resulted in an intimidating relationship for many men. But evidently not for Jethro. At some point in God's assignments, Moses had sent his wife and two sons back to live with the in-laws until life was at a less taxing place. When Jethro heard about the success of the Exodus and the Israelites' escape from Pharaoh, he took his daughter and two grandsons to see Moses, sending a message ahead to say they were coming.

After his family arrived at the Israelite camp near the Mountain of God and they had greeted one another, Moses shared with Jethro all the details of what God had done since they had last been together. Imagine how amazing that must have been to sit and listen to Moses recall the entire story of the battle with Pharaoh directly and personally in his own words. Jethro's response was of great gratitude, so he brought offerings and sacrifices to God as the elders of Israel joined him.

The next day, Moses went to work to carry out his usual job of taking a seat to hear and settle issues among the people. People waited in line all day to stand before Moses. As Jethro watched this excruciatingly slow parade looking for counsel and intervention in many areas, he did what any good father-in-law would do: offered a better plan.

He questioned Moses on what the point was in all this work and why he was taking it on alone with no help. The bottom line of Moses' answer was that he spoke for God and the people were all aware of that fact. So out of protection for his son-in-law, whom he loved and respected, coupled with his concern for the weary people waiting in line, Jethro warned Moses of the eventual consequences but then offered a God-inspired alternative.

"This is not good!" Moses' father-in-law exclaimed. "You're going to wear yourself out—and the people, too. This job is too heavy a burden for you to handle all by yourself. Now listen to me, and let me give you a word of advice, and may God be with you. You should continue to be the people's representative before God, bringing their disputes to him. Teach them God's decrees, and give them his instructions. Show them how to conduct their lives." (Exodus 18:17–20)

A good leader knows you can't just present a problem and restate the obvious goal. You need to bring a solution and a viable plan to consider. Jethro did just that.

"But select from all the people some capable, honest men who fear God and hate bribes. Appoint them as leaders over groups of one thousand, one hundred, fifty, and ten. They should always be

available to solve the people's common disputes, but have them bring the major cases to you. Let the leaders decide the smaller matters themselves. They will help you carry the load, making the task easier for you. If you follow this advice, and if God commands you to do so, then you will be able to endure the pressures, and all these people will go home in peace." (Exodus 18:21–23)

Essentially Jethro described to his son-in-law the type of man he needed and then the specific structure to build around him and those key men. Feeling mutual respect for his father-in-law and knowing his heart for him and the nation, Moses listened intently, took the wisdom, agreed, and followed the plan to the letter. He sought out the right men, appointed them as leaders and gave them authority, and put them in charge of groups ranging from one thousand down to ten, depending on the needs. The men stepped up to the challenge and took on their new duties with great success.

We can see from this description that the judicial systems of the ages are copies of this first governmental court system to hear grievances and offer judgments. Through his outside assessment and wisdom acting as an ancient-day efficiency expert, Jethro brought balance to Moses and the entire nation.

Has there been a time when God used a family member or close friend to change your life by offering solid wisdom or godly counsel? Explain.

_____

_____

_____

_____

_____

Has God ever allowed you the opportunity to change the life of a family member or close friend with your advice and counsel from Him? Explain.

_____

_____

_____

_____

_____

"Heavenly Father, thank You for Your flow chart of authority and how You have provided systems and plans for the practical and physical aspects of this life. Grant me the wisdom to listen to others who speak into my life from You, while I also listen and give to others for Your glory. In Jesus' name, amen."

MEMORY VERSE

WITHOUT WISE LEADERSHIP, A NATION FALLS;
THERE IS SAFETY IN HAVING MANY ADVISERS.

- PROVERBS 11:14 -

LEADERS DELEGATE, MEDIATE, EDUCATE, NAVIGATE, EVALUATE, MOTIVATE, AND ELEVATE.

While the world offers many paths, *God* offers one — HIS.

JOSHUA
PREPARED

JOSHUA 24

Joshua had stood in Moses' shadow and sacrificially served the nation's leader, but then his turn came and God promoted him to the top spot. He had been faithful in the little things, so now God could trust him to be faithful in much (see Luke 16:10). He had followed well, and was now prepared and ready to lead well. But Joshua had a skill for Israel's next steps as a nation that Moses was not equipped for. Joshua was a battle-ready warrior when his name was called to step out front.

Well after the fall of Jericho and the many other conquests, when Joshua was much older, he gathered all the tribes together at Shechem to present the people to the Lord. He had heard from God and spoke with boldness, reminding them all of God's great acts throughout their history, right up to their present day. He summed up his challenge from the Lord with these words:

"So fear the Lord. Serve Him in faith and truth. Put away the gods your fathers served on the other side of the river and in Egypt. Serve the Lord. If you think it is wrong to serve the Lord, choose today whom you will serve. Choose the gods your fathers worshiped on the other side of the river, or choose the gods of

the Amorites in whose land you are living. But as for me and my
family, we will serve the Lord." (Joshua 24:14–15 NLV)

Joshua drew a spiritual line in the sand and told each family to choose a side. The God or gods? Immanuel or idols? Time for everyone to decide. Follow the path of disobedience of your ancestors, or decide on obedience for yourself today with no turning back? Joshua then made his own family's choice quite clear, and the words have been memorialized in thousands of different ways throughout history.

Whether you come from a horrible home or the perfect family, the true guiding biblical principle of Joshua's challenge today is that you get to choose your own direction and destination. No matter if you came from a legacy of devastating dysfunction or a happily-ever-after story, you can make the decision to serve the Lord for the rest of your days.

In a very real way, Joshua shouted God's message out to the generations of the world and to every family for all time until Christ's triumphant return.

In a relationship with God through Christ, you can choose to be a leader today. Whether you feel as though you constantly fail or you are just walking through a difficult season, submission to the Lord can change *everything*. Your level of spiritual maturity depends solely on the depth of your obedience. You can accelerate your growth to be prepared and to experience victory in your life.

That is exactly why you can find a man who has been in church for forty years yet has little to no ability to lead and disciple others, while another man who has been a Christ-follower for only five years has become an amazing role model. Because the latter has dug deep in his obedience.

As men who follow Christ, we must stay prepared, exactly as Joshua's life displays, to be alert and available to anything God needs from us and has for us.

The toughest circumstance that God has used in my life to prepare me for His work is:

_____

_____

_____

_____

Today, I believe God has me prepared in the area of:

_____

_____

_____

_____

because ultimately He wants me to:

_____

_____

_____

_____

"Heavenly Father, thank You that every day I can choose to follow Joshua's example and heed his words to serve You and You alone. Give me the strength and courage to stay alert and available to You, prepared for anything that You may call me to take on in Your name for Your glory. In Jesus' name, amen."

MEMORY VERSE

Write your name in the blank to personalize and memorize this adaptation of today's verse:

BUT AS FOR _____

AND MY FAMILY, WE WILL SERVE THE LORD.

- JOSHUA 24:15 NLV, ADAPTED -

THE CHAPTERS FROM YOUR PAST
ARE FOR THE CHALLENGES YOU FACE TODAY
FOR THE CHARACTER YOU WILL HAVE TOMORROW.

NO MATTER where you come from, God CAN GET YOU where YOU need to go.

SHAMGAR
RESOURCEFUL

JUDGES 3:31

Throughout the Bible there are men whose names we find in only one verse. Sometimes the context of their story leaves a horrible legacy of evil, while others paint an incredibly impressive picture that would make any man proud.

One such name with a very short story is Shamgar.

After Ehud, Shamgar son of Anath rescued Israel. He once killed 600 Philistines with an ox goad. (Judges 3:31)

The first sentence sets up his lineage and legacy in Israel's history book. But the second sentence is a one-line description for an action film! He singlehandedly took out six hundred Philistine warriors with a *what*? The New Life Bible's version of the same verse offers a simple, modern explanation:

After Ehud, Shamgar the son of Anath became the leader. He killed 600 Philistines with a stick used to push cattle, and he also saved Israel.

Just before this verse, we read that Israel had defeated Moab by killing ten thousand of their strongest and most able-bodied warriors in the final battle. Verse 30 closes with "and there was peace in the land for eighty years."

Theologians tell us that Israel began to struggle through a depressed economic state. The Philistines, who would become an ongoing enemy of Israel, started invasions to take advantage of their dire circumstances. They knew that at the time, the Israelites were totally unprepared for war. Upon one particular attack, Shamgar took matters into his own hands—literally—choosing a common tool of a farmer to fight.

The reality is there are times when it does not matter *what* is in a man's hands, but rather *whose* hands it is in. The right man for the job, with the right skill and mindset, can become very resourceful when a crisis arises.

The ox goad, or cattle prod, was a pole up to ten feet long with one end sharpened, used to herd oxen and cattle in the right direction. Imagine a man wielding that glorified "stick," as the NLV calls it, to kill six hundred men! You can envision him spinning the pole full speed like a Jedi knight wielding his light saber, taking out bad guys by the dozens as they ran at him from all sides.

Two fascinating points emerge in this one verse proving Shamgar's obviously brave resourcefulness:

1. He used a tool of the local trade as a weapon of war to save God's people.

2. He did all he could, with what he had, right where he was.

The Bible is clear that as Christ-followers, we are called to accomplish God's work between salvation and Heaven. We are eternally accountable to Him in our obedience.

Following Shamgar's principle, our tools of the trade can become weapons of war in the spiritual battle for souls. Following his example, we can do all we can with what we have right where we are for God's glory.

A doctor can spend Saturdays at a homeless shelter treating the sick. A construction foreman can fix the rundown homes of the elderly. An attorney can provide pro bono work to inmates to prove their innocence. A writer can create Gospel resources. A police officer can volunteer as security at his church. An accountant can help single moms get their taxes done and maximize finances. A musician can write and record songs that encourage people.

The key in all these examples is to fulfill Jesus' words in Matthew 25:40: *"I tell you the truth, when you did it to one of the least of these my brothers and sisters, you were doing it to me!"* We use our God-given resources to battle the Enemy's work in the world by sharing Christ and serving in His name.

A "Shamgar moment" when I know God empowered me to do battle for Him was:

_____

_____

_____

_____

_____

I believe God is calling me to use my (tools of the trade):

_____

_____

_____

as His weapon of war to:

_____

_____

_____

"Heavenly Father, thank You for my tools of the trade that I can use for You and Your Kingdom. Give me a vision for how I can turn more of my talents and skills over to You. Please prepare and empower me to do all I can with what I have right where I am in Your name for Your glory. In Jesus' name, amen."

MEMORY VERSE

" 'I TELL YOU THE TRUTH,
WHEN YOU DID IT TO ONE OF THE LEAST OF THESE
MY BROTHERS AND SISTERS,
YOU WERE DOING IT TO ME!' '

- MATTHEW 25:40 -

NO MATTER THE LIMITATIONS OF THE MOMENT, USE ALL YOUR AVAILABLE RESOURCES, AND NEVER OFFER EXCUSES.

DO *all you can* with **what you have,** RIGHT WHERE YOU ARE, all for *God's glory.*

Judges 6 starts out with the Israelites hiding in caves in the mountains. Their enemy at the time was the Midianites, who would attack and take everything from crops to livestock. Israel was starving and once again cried out to God for His help.

Gideon had set up a threshing floor for wheat in an abandoned winepress. Normally wheat was threshed out in the open up on a hill so the wind could naturally blow away the chaff, but inside, he could stay hidden as well as protect his food source from the enemy.

The angel of the Lord appeared to him and said, "Mighty hero, the Lord is with you!" ... "But Lord," Gideon replied, "how can I rescue Israel? My clan is the weakest in the whole tribe of Manasseh, and I am the least in my entire family!" The Lord said to him, "I will be with you. And you will destroy the Midianites as if you were fighting against one man." (Judges 6:12, 15–16)

A principle we regularly see in Scripture is that God often chooses the guy who believes he is last in line for anything. Gideon certainly made his lack of belief in himself clear. He declared himself a *wimp* when God saw a *warrior*. When we adopt this same mind-set about ourselves, we must remember Gideon's story.

Fast-forward to Judges 7. Theologians believe that the Midian-ite raiding parties numbered over one hundred thousand strong. Gideon had managed to pull together an army about a third the size—but God was about to create some interesting math with his new warrior leader.

With thirty-two thousand men, God told Gideon he had *too many* warriors because if they won even at three-to-one odds, they would take the glory for themselves. So Gideon announced that if anyone was afraid, they could leave and go home with no con-sequences. And twenty-two thousand guys got up and walked away, leaving ten thousand.

When the dust settled, God again told Gideon that there were too many warriors. He gave instructions of a crazy way to cull them, and three hundred passed the God test. From thirty-two thousand down to three hundred. God essentially said, "Okay, you're good now. You'll win." Little did Gideon know that God had devised a plan where not a single Israelite would do battle.

When the 300 Israelites blew their rams' horns, the LORD caused the warriors in the camp to fight against each other with their swords. Those who were not killed fled to places as far away as Beth-shittah near Zererah and to the border of Abel-meholah near Tabbath. (Judges 7:22)

Here are five principles to glean from Gideon's story:

1. Where the world often sees a wimp, God can see a warrior.
2. The people who feel last on the list, God can choose to be first.
3. God's math and the world's math never match up.
4. To win a battle, God only asks for availability, not ability.
5. When God leads the charge, the battle is always won.

There are seasons in life when we start to believe that we must have certain people on our team to win a battle. Or we think a certain goal can be reached only by a certain number of people. Using Gideon's opening scene as an analogy, we can also be hiding in fear in the winepress when we should be up on the hill threshing in faith.

Spiritual maturity brings us to the place where we stop telling God what we must have before we will fight the battle, and start asking Him what He wants from us to win. The key is found in Judges 6:16: "The Lord said to him, 'I will be with you.'"

The first time I felt God call me out of hiding to be His warrior was:

_____

_____

_____

_____

_____

_____

The battle I am facing right now where I feel the odds are against me and need God to come through is:

_____

_____

_____

_____

_____

_____

"Heavenly Father, thank You for all the times I felt last on the list, but You brought me to the front, even though I thought I was a wimp and not a warrior. Remind me, when I start focusing on my ability, that You only need my availability. I want to face the battles in this world with only You. In Jesus' name, amen."

MEMORY VERSE

Write your name in the blank to personalize and memorize this adaptation of today's verse:

THE LORD SAID TO

_____

"I WILL BE WITH YOU."

- JUDGES 6:16, ADAPTED -

THE RIGHT TEAM IS NEVER ABOUT QUANTITY,
BUT QUALITY, NOT THE NUMBERS,
BUT THE NAMES ON THE ROSTER.

GOD requires you to LEAVE THE comfort zone before you can walk into the winner's CIRCLE.

Only four chapters long, the book of Ruth is an inspiring story of God leading two people to discover great love. And against all the cultural bias of that day, God made sure this particular book in His Word was named after the woman, not the man. That intentional approach reveals His heart toward the character, commitment, and compassion of this amazing woman. But because of the nature of the story, we can easily overlook the amazing qualities of Boaz just as we do some other men in Scripture.

The one striking characteristic this man showed to Ruth throughout the story is chivalry. Because of confused and chaotic cultural norms today, along with blurred lines between masculinity and femininity, chivalry seems to be a dying art. Chivalry can simply be defined as being a gentleman in your conduct, particularly when expressed to women. That is precisely why, as men who follow Christ, we must stay focused on this necessary and much-needed quality.

Ruth's mother-in-law, Naomi, had legally released her daughter-in-law from any family responsibility, but Ruth's commitment to her late husband and his family remained faithful, regardless of their dire circumstances. We are then introduced to Boaz as a wealthy, influential, and respected man in the community. He was a good man with a good name.

As Ruth went out alone to try to gather food for herself and Naomi, she came in behind the harvesters in Boaz's field to gather the grain left behind on the ground. Boaz saw Ruth, and rather than have someone chase her away as would often occur in those days, he went out to tell her to stay only in his field for both her protection and provision. He knew that a single, attractive young woman out alone could quickly fall into trouble. Boaz instructed his workers to let her glean and to also share their food and water that he had provided. Ruth was so surprised by his generosity that her response reflected her heart.

Ruth fell at his feet and thanked him warmly. "What have I done to deserve such kindness?" she asked. "I am only a foreigner." "Yes, I know," Boaz replied. "But I also know about everything you have done for your mother-in-law since the death of your husband. I have heard how you left your father and mother and your own land to live here among complete strangers. May the LORD, the God of Israel, under whose wings you have come to take refuge, reward you fully for what you have done." "I hope I continue to please you, sir," she replied. "You have comforted me by speaking so kindly to me." (Ruth 2:10–13)

Ruth and Boaz were from completely different countries, backgrounds, and economic circumstances, but their strong characters and common qualities drew them together. Both their public reputations preceded them; Boaz had already heard of Ruth's sacrifice and service to her husband's family. When he saw her in his field, he knew the kind of woman she was. Throughout their short love story captured in Scripture, both of them kept proving their loving commitment to God, others, and one another. Their like minds and hearts led them to fall in love and get married.

Throughout the story, Boaz always put Ruth first. He considered her needs and provided for her and Naomi. He was careful to honor and protect her good name and reputation. He followed the protocols of the community to legally seek her hand in marriage. (Boaz and Ruth's son was King David's grandfather, placing them in the lineage of Jesus.)

To close this day, here's a great story to express how we should view chivalry: A man walked up to the large glass doors of a corporate building at the same time that a female executive approached. He opened the door wide, stepped back, smiled, and motioned for her to walk in ahead of him. She immediately stopped, glared at him, and blurted out, "You're only opening the door for me because I am a woman, aren't you?" The man calmly answered, "No, ma'am. I'm opening the door for you because I am a gentleman."

The man's actions were not determined by *her gender*, but by *his nature*.

My relationship with Christ has most affected my view of women by/in:

_____

_____

_____

_____

_____

One way I know I can continue to grow and lead in chivalry is to:

_____

_____

_____

_____

_____

_____

"Lord Jesus, when You were here, You always showed great respect toward women and showed no bias or inequality. You honored them all, from Your own mother to the woman at the well. Help me to show that same respect through chivalry to all women, young and old, the powerful to the poor. In Jesus' name, amen."

MEMORY VERSE

Treat older women as you would your mother, and treat younger women with all purity as you would your own sisters.

- 1 Timothy 5:2 -

TREAT EVERYONE AS EQUALS,
NOT BECAUSE OF WHO THEY ARE,
BUT BECAUSE OF WHO YOU ARE.

Chivalry
is a response of
respect—
NOT RANDOM ACTS,
but redeemed proactivity.

SAMUEL
RELIABLE

1 SAMUEL 1–3

Today is not about a man, but a boy. An amazing boy. When Samuel's mother had been at the Temple praying, Eli had blessed her with the child she had been praying for. Then, when Samuel was weaned from her, out of gratitude she took him back to Eli and gave the boy up for service there: "Now I am giving him to the LORD, and he will belong to the LORD his whole life" (1 Samuel 1:28). In Samuel 2:26, we read, "Meanwhile, the boy Samuel grew taller and grew in favor with the LORD and with the people." We have seen this type of language used to describe Noah and Joseph as well.

One night, Eli and Samuel were asleep in the Temple—Eli in his quarters and Samuel near the Ark of the Covenant of God. Suddenly, Samuel heard someone call his name. The boy got up and ran to Eli and said, "Here I am. You called me." Eli, surprised, said, "I did not call you. Go back and lie down." Samuel, a little confused, obeyed.

Again the boy heard, "Samuel!" So he got up and went to Eli again, and said, "Here I am. You called me." Yet again, Eli said, "My son, I did not call. Now go back and lie down."

Finally a third time, Samuel heard his name called out. Puzzled but trying to be obedient to his master, the boy got up, went to Eli, and repeated, "Here I am. You called me." In that moment, Eli realized that God had called Samuel, so he told the boy, "Go and lie down, and if God calls you again, answer, 'Speak, Lord, Your servant is listening.'"

This time Samuel did exactly what Eli had told him, and answered, "Speak, Lord, Your servant is listening." Scripture indicates that this was not an angel talking to Samuel, but the Lord Himself.

This story has a combination of intrigue, mystery, and even a little comedy, as Samuel kept hearing his name and going to Eli. God delivered a message of judgment regarding Eli and his disobedient sons, and Eli's response and the close of the story of Samuel's growth into adulthood as a servant of God is amazing and inspiring.

But Eli called out to him, "Samuel, my son." "Here I am," Samuel replied. "What did the LORD say to you? Tell me everything. And may God strike you and even kill you if you hide anything from me!" So Samuel told Eli everything; he didn't hold anything back. "It is the LORD's will," Eli replied. "Let him do what he thinks best." As Samuel grew up, the LORD was with him, and everything Samuel said proved to be reliable. And all Israel, from Dan in the north to Beersheba in the south, knew that Samuel was confirmed as a prophet of the LORD. The LORD continued to

appear at Shiloh and gave messages to Samuel there at the Tab-
ernacle. (1 Samuel 3:16–20)

Take a look at these truths we can glean from this passage:

- Samuel was 100 percent honest to deliver God's message.
- Eli fully trusted Samuel's words as from God.
- Everything Samuel said proved reliable.
- All of Israel deemed Samuel a prophet of God.
- God kept speaking to Samuel in the Tabernacle for the entire nation.
- Samuel kept listening to God and always heard Him.

When we talk about prayer and a relationship with God, we tend to focus on what *we* say. We can spend a great deal of time trying to "do the right thing" to try to get God to respond to our prayers. The greatest principle we can take from Samuel's young life is how crucial it is for us to listen to God. Take the time in your own prayers to invite Him to speak and then listen to Him when He does speak. Psalm 46:10 offers a great way to begin to listen: "Be still, and know that I am God!"

The last time I knew for certain I heard God speak to my spirit was:

_____

_____

_____

_____

_____

_____

The situation in my life right now that I really need to hear God's voice is:

_____

_____

_____

_____

_____

_____

"Heavenly Father, thank You that a relationship with You means that You can and will speak to me. Help me to listen, tune in, and hear anything You say to me. Help me to be found as reliable as Samuel to hear from You and do what You tell me. Speak, Lord, Your servant is listening. In Jesus' name, amen."

MEMORY VERSE

Write your name in the blank to personalize and memorize this adaptation of today's verse:

SPEAK, LORD, YOUR SERVANT

IS LISTENING.

- 1 SAMUEL 3:9, ADAPTED -

**PROACTIVE AND INTENTIONAL LISTENING
IS A CRITICAL AND CRUCIAL
CHARACTERISTIC OF LEADERSHIP.**

GOD
desires to speak to
HIS PEOPLE,
BUT HE MUST FIRST HAVE
someone willing
to take the time to
listen to Him.

JONATHAN
LOYAL

1 SAMUEL 14, 19

Tracking Jonathan's life in Scripture, we see time and time again how he:

- Was loyal to God
- Had loyalty to others
- Returned loyalty from others

In 1 Samuel 14, King Saul and six hundred men were at a standstill and camped out because the Philistine army had gained control of the pass through the mountains. Jonathan decided to take action without telling his dad.

"Let's go across to the outpost of those pagans," Jonathan said to his armor bearer. "Perhaps the LORD will help us, for nothing can hinder the LORD. He can win a battle whether he has many warriors or only a few!" "Do what you think is best," the armor bearer replied. "I'm with you completely, whatever you decide." (1 Samuel 14:6–7)

Clearly, Jonathan had come to an understanding of God that resulted in his belief in the One who will fight and win the battle when He has faithful warriors. In this case, knowing the odds, Jonathan believed that $2 + God > 600$ Philistines. By his positive response, the armor bearer had obvious faith in and loyalty to both Jonathan *and* God.

After devising a strategy of attack with the help of the Lord, Jonathan and his armor bearer climbed up the cliff—free-solo style, no ropes, only their hands and feet. In the first advance, the two warriors killed twenty men. Then God showed up as panic struck the entire Philistine army, along with an earthquake. Suddenly the enemy wasn't very concerned with the two Israelite warriors. Saul realized something was happening and called his army to action. They gave chase as the Philistines ran away. Once again, we see how God used a faithful few to save the nation and rout an overwhelming enemy.

Following this event, Saul's poor leadership yet again created another national issue. Trying to evade the consequences, Saul was backed into a corner and threatened his own son's life. But then Jonathan reaped what he had sown for God and the nation.

But the people broke in and said to Saul, "Jonathan has won this great victory for Israel. Should he die? Far from it! As surely as the LORD lives, not one hair on his head will be touched, for God helped him do a great deed today." So the people rescued Jonathan, and he was not put to death. (1 Samuel 14:45)

After God rejected Saul and introduced David into the picture, and the battle with Goliath occurred, Saul's jealousy raged. Jonathan worked hard to be loyal to his father as king, but also to his new friend and future king. When Saul ordered his son to kill David, Jonathan again risked his life for God and the nation.

"The king must not sin against his servant David," Jonathan said. "He's never done anything to harm you. He has always helped you in any way he could. Have you forgotten about the time he risked his life to kill the Philistine giant and how the LORD brought a great victory to all Israel as a result? You were certainly happy about it then. Why should you murder an innocent man like David? There is no reason for it at all!" So Saul listened to Jonathan and vowed, "As surely as the LORD lives, David will not be killed." Afterward Jonathan called David and told him what had happened. Then he brought David to Saul, and David served in the court as before. (1 Samuel 19:4–7)

Obviously, much of the focus in these chapters is on Saul and David. But we must not miss the amazing people God used to intervene, connect, and bring about His will. Jonathan may have always lived in the shadows of his dad and best friend, but he should definitely be on our list of men from whom we can gain inspiration and motivation in our walk with God.

I tend to struggle with being loyal when:

_____

_____

_____

I tend to be loyal when:

_____

_____

The relationships in my life in which I believe
God has called me to be loyal are:

_____   _____

_____   _____

_____   _____

_____   _____

_____   _____

"Heavenly Father, Your loyalty to the Israelites was so faithful, no matter what they did. Your loyalty to mankind in sending your Son while we were still sinners is beyond understanding. Your loyalty to me throughout my life to bless, provide, save, protect, and sustain me is more than I can imagine. Help me to grow in my loyalty, first to You, and second to those You place in my life. In Jesus' name, amen."

MEMORY VERSE

Memorize Jonathan's armor bearer's
pledge as your own daily prayer to God.

*"DO WHAT YOU THINK IS BEST …
I'M WITH YOU COMPLETELY, WHATEVER YOU DECIDE."*

- 1 SAMUEL 14:7 -

TRUE LOYALTY IS NOT BLIND,
BUT RATHER SEES THE TRUTH
THROUGH GRACE.

Christ-like
LOYALTY
ALWAYS BELIEVES FOR THE
BEST
& WON'T
give up
on the worst.

DAVID
PASSIONATE

1 SAMUEL 16–17, 2 SAMUEL 11–12, PSALM 51

As a young shepherd boy, David was well trained after being left alone for long periods of time with the family's flocks of sheep. He had to singlehandedly fight off bears and lions to keep them from eating the sheep—and, of course, him. From his experience in the field and his deep faith in God, he became a tough, gutsy young man.

When his father sent him to the front lines to take food to his brothers, David quickly heard about this giant named Goliath who was taunting the nation and his God. Confused and frustrated as to why everyone was so afraid of just one huge loudmouth, David decided to take care of the standoff—just like he had gone after the predators who had come to attack his sheep. (Once again, a metaphor of God's people.)

After Goliath's taunting and an exchange of words between him and David, the shepherd-warrior ran at the giant and nailed him in the forehead with a rock. Then he grabbed Goliath's massive sword and cut his head off. Problem solved.

The nation saved. God glorified.

To no one's surprise, David later became king. Then, after a long streak of success as a conqueror, one spring he decided to stay home while his army went out. One bored afternoon strolling on his roof, high above all the houses, he saw a beautiful woman nearby, bathing in her courtyard. Temptation got the best of him and he sent for her. Problem started.

A nation jeopardized. God ignored.

After the woman named Bathsheba told David she was pregnant, he set off on a mission to cover his tracks that led to manipulation and the murder of her husband. God used Nathan the prophet to get through to David using the story of a poor man's pet lamb that related back to David's heart for his flock where he first learned to trust God. While David's initial response to Nathan's parable was an anger-fueled fit of rage that demanded immediate justice, the prophet connected the dots to the king's sin and God's call for repentance.

The words of Psalm 51 came out of the same heart that protected the sheep and took care of Goliath. David's passion turned inward to reflect the brokenness of his heart for his sin and desire for restoration with God.

Have mercy on me, O God, because of your unfailing love. Because of your great compassion, blot out the stain of my sins. Wash me clean from my guilt. Purify me from my sin. For I recognize my rebellion; it haunts me day and night. Against you, and you alone, have I sinned; I have done what is evil in your sight. ... Restore to me the joy of your salvation, and make me willing to obey you. Then I will teach your ways to rebels, and they will return to you. Forgive me for shedding blood, O God who saves; then I will joyfully sing of your forgiveness. Unseal my lips, O LORD, that my mouth may praise you. (Psalm 51:1–4, 12–15)

David invited God to do what only He can do when we have seen the worst of what we can do in our sin. God has to work on us, then in us, before He can work through us. This is what happens when a loving, merciful, persistent, grace-filled God intervenes in the life of a dysfunctional, issue-ridden, self-centered man. Redemption, forgiveness, healing, salvation, and restoration occur. Righteousness meets rebellion, and wrongs are made right. David's passion for God is seen throughout his life, whether he was a conquering king or broken sinner.

My "solo shepherd season" where God first trained me to trust Him and express my faith was:

_____

_____

_____

_____

_____

_____

My deepest moment of brokenness that God used to humble and prepare me for ministry to others was:

_____

_____

_____

_____

_____

_____

"Heavenly Father, You called David 'a man after my own heart that will do everything I want him to do.' Even after horrible sin, You restored and redeemed his life. His honest writings in Psalms show us his passion to love and serve You. God, help me to be that kind of man. Help me to have that kind of heart for You. In Jesus' name, amen."

MEMORY VERSE

Write your name in the blank to personalize and memorize this adaptation of today's verse:

"I HAVE FOUND

_____

A MAN AFTER MY OWN HEART.
HE WILL DO EVERYTHING I WANT HIM TO DO."

- ACTS 13:22, ADAPTED -

PASSION IN A MAN'S HEART
IS NEVER TAUGHT,
BUT CAUGHT.

A MAN
after
God's heart
KEEPS THE

FOCUS ON OBEDIENCE,
NOT
OBSTACLES.

NATHAN
BOLDNESS

2 SAMUEL 7, 12

In 2 Samuel 7, we first read about Nathan the prophet regarding David's concern for building God a proper home to keep the Ark of the Covenant. The king wanted to move God from a tent to a temple, but Nathan heard from the Lord that God would build David's house and then his son (Solomon) would be the leader to build the temple.

Connecting back to yesterday's story of David and Bathsheba, let's look closer at Nathan's role in David's repentance. The focus is the risky gut-level honesty with which Nathan confronted the king.

Second Samuel 12 begins by stating clearly that God sent Nathan to David. Nathan had no agenda and wasn't after David to prove a point or call him out. The prophet was merely doing God's business and being His messenger, which, sometimes, is not about delivering good news.

As Nathan told the story, we don't know whether David heard this as a parable or an actual account. Nathan told the king that there were two men in the same town, one rich and one poor. The wealthy man had many head of sheep and cattle. The poor man owned only one little lamb that was dearly loved by his family and was treated as a pet, not livestock to be eaten or sold.

When the rich man wanted to entertain a guest, rather than get one of his many animals to butcher and serve, he took the poor man's lamb. Because of David's history as a shepherd who loved and protected his sheep, this story pulled his heartstrings in a major way. David demanded repayment and restitution four-fold and then, to finish off the culprit, the death sentence. No grace and no mercy for such an act.

While we do not know if Nathan knew David well enough to predict such a story would create such a strong response, God certainly did. And again, God sent Nathan and he delivered the message with clarity. The most intriguing part of this account is what happened next in Nathan's response to David.

Then Nathan said to David, "You are that man! The LORD, the God of Israel, says: I anointed you king of Israel and saved you from the power of Saul. I gave you your master's house and his wives and the kingdoms of Israel and Judah. And if that had not been enough, I would have given you much, much more. Why, then, have you despised the word of the LORD and done this horrible deed? For you have murdered Uriah the Hittite with the sword of the Ammonites and stolen his wife. From this time on, your family will live by the sword because you have despised me by taking Uriah's wife to be your own. This is what the LORD says: Because of what you have done, I will cause your own household to rebel against you. I will give your wives to another man before your very eyes, and he will go to bed with them in public view. You did it secretly, but I will make this happen to you openly in the sight of all Israel." (2 Samuel 12:7–12)

We cannot miss the fact that David was a powerful king and a skilled warrior. Many kings would have executed such a messenger immediately, especially in such a heightened moment of emotion that incited shame and embarrassment. We must also pay attention to Nathan's words and point of view. He spoke completely and only from God's perspective. From the prophet's mouth came accusation, judgment, and pronouncement of a verdict and sentence, all in direct first person. But verse 13, the very next sentence, revealed the king's response:

Then David confessed to Nathan, "I have sinned against the LORD."

David realized that the firsthand knowledge came from God's heart through Nathan's mouth. The great risk Nathan took to obey God and confront the king ended in the full repentance of one of the key pillars in the foundation of the lineage of Jesus. Nathan heard from God, acted upon the call, and saw the fruit of his obedience right away. From a major mess, Nathan brought powerful ministry. Out of Nathan's risking his life, God brought new life. From a web of lies, Nathan weaved God's truth into the story.

When God asks me to speak truth in any circumstance, my biggest struggle tends to be:

_____

_____

_____

_____

_____

_____

My most challenging moment when God had me to present His truth was:

_____

_____

_____

_____

_____

_____

"Heavenly Father, in our politically correct world, speaking Your truth is challenging and risky. Help me to balance showing Your love with speaking Your truth. Give me strength and boldness to communicate whatever You call on me to speak. In Jesus' name, amen."

MEMORY VERSE

Write your name in the blank to personalize and memorize this adaptation of today's verse:

AND NOW, O LORD, ... GIVE

_____

YOUR SERVANT, GREAT BOLDNESS IN

PREACHING YOUR WORD.

- ACTS 4:29, ADAPTED -

**BOLDNESS IS BEST EXPRESSED
AFTER BEING TEMPERED
IN THE FLAMES OF BROKENNESS.**

The wicked run away
when no one is chasing them,
but the *godly*

ARE AS BOLD AS LIONS.

PROVERBS 28:1

MEPHIBOSHETH
RESTORED

2 SAMUEL 9

From biblical to medieval times, when a new king would come into power from a different family lineage, a common practice was to kill off any family members left from the old regime. This tactic aimed to prevent any possibility of a family member attempting to gain support to overthrow the throne.

After Saul died, David had finally taken over and led Israel to great military success. David began to think about Saul's family and wondered if anyone remained. Because of his loyalty to and friendship with Jonathan, David inquired about any members still alive. He learned that one of Jonathan's sons (Saul's grandson) lived in an impoverished town called Lo-debar. David sent for him to be brought to the palace. The young man's name was Mephibosheth, and he had been crippled since he was very young.

Imagine for a moment when Mephibosheth was told that King David had sent someone from Jerusalem to bring him before the throne. The natural assumption would be that David intended to execute him. The trip to the capital would have been full of fear and dread.

When he came to David, he bowed low to the ground in deep respect. David said, "Greetings, Mephibosheth." Mephibosheth replied, "I am your servant." "Don't be afraid!" David said. "I intend to show kindness to you because of my promise to your father, Jonathan. I will give you all the property that once belonged to your grandfather Saul, and you will eat here with me at the king's table!" Mephibosheth bowed respectfully and exclaimed, "Who is your servant, that you should show such kindness to a dead dog like me?" Then the king summoned Saul's servant Ziba and said, "I have given your master's grandson everything that belonged to Saul and his family. You and your sons and servants are to farm the land for him to produce food for your master's household." (2 Samuel 9:6–10)

Mephibosheth allowed us to see into his heart when he called himself a "dead dog." He lived in poverty in a small, disrespected town with nothing left from his grandfather and father's estate. He was crippled, so he couldn't work, and there was a strong likelihood he could not walk on his own or would have certainly struggled to do so. If so, in that day he would have had to be carried or crawl anywhere he needed to go. Imagine for a moment being in such a constantly desperate situation living in such a humbled state.

But then something happened no one saw coming. The king gave back everything that his family owned, set up an income for him, and then invited him to eat at his table every night—a table to which he potentially would have to be carried.

Friends, that is the very picture of what King Jesus does for us in salvation, redemption, and sanctification. We deserve death because of our "family line" of sin. But He brings us before His throne and makes us His own, sets up a new life for us, and invites us to His table from now into eternity. Because of our past, our sin, and our brokenness, we too are crippled. But in our desperate and dependent state, Jesus carries us to His table to live and fellowship with Him.

And Mephibosheth, who was crippled in both feet, lived in Jerusalem and ate regularly at the king's table. (2 Samuel 9:13)

Today, regardless of your past failures, mistakes, and choices, God invites you to His table through a relationship with Jesus Christ. And if you aren't sure if or don't feel like you can pull yourself to the table, He will carry you.

That is how God sees us. That is what God offers us. That is what God will do for us.

When I first realized my sin and knew I needed Jesus to save me, I remember feeling:

_____

_____

_____

_____

_____

_____

I feel the most gratitude for Christ's salvation, constant forgiveness of my sin, and continual restoration of my life when:

_____

_____

_____

_____

_____

_____

"Heavenly Father, thank You that, like David to Mephibosheth, You came after me, brought me to You, saved, restored, and forgave me, and now You invite me to fellowship at Your table. Thank You for Your gift of salvation and restoration. In Jesus' name, amen."

MEMORY VERSE

Write your name in the blank to personalize and memorize this adaptation of today's verse:

WHEN

_____

[WAS] UTTERLY HELPLESS, CHRIST CAME AT JUST THE RIGHT TIME AND DIED FOR [HIM].

ROMANS 5:6, ADAPTED -

**THE BEST LEADER TO FOLLOW
INTO A FIRE IS ONE WHO
HAS BEEN THROUGH A FIRE.**

When we are too crippled to walk,
God will carry us
into
His presence.

DAY 15

BENAIAH
PROACTIVE

2 SAMUEL 8:18, 20:23, 23:20

1 CHRONICLES 11:23-24, 27:5-6

Benaiah has some of the most impressive moments in the Bible that are also some of the shortest. Even though the passages about him are brief, the stories are epic. The first mention of him in 2 Samuel 8 and 20 tell us he was captain of King David's bodyguards.

In a section titled "David's Thirty Mighty Men," Benaiah is one of only two warriors who have details written about them before the roster of the other twenty-eight men is given. (An interesting note is that Bathsheba's husband Uriah is the last name on the list.) These warriors were known for their great skill in battle and bravery; they are legends in Israel's history. In a day of predominantly hand-to-hand combat, being a man known for many victories that honor the king and the nation was impressive.

Check out this résumé for the bodyguard of the king:

Benaiah son of Jehoiada, a valiant fighter from Kabzeel, performed great exploits. He struck down Moab's two mightiest war-

*riors. He also went down into a pit on a snowy day and killed a
lion. (2 Samuel 23:20 NIV)*

Battling Moab's two main men makes sense from a military
standpoint, but we aren't told why Benaiah went after the lion.
Was the predator being a threat to the area? Was he seeking revenge because a friend was attacked? Or was it just a matter of
sport because he could? Regardless of the motive, making the
conscious decision to pursue a lion down into a pit and take him
out alone is like a scene from an action film. And a snowy day
indicates winter. Everything is harder when its freezing cold,
which adds another amazing detail.

One other passage records Benaiah's skill as a warrior:

*Once, armed only with a club, he killed an Egyptian warrior who
was 7 1/2 feet tall and who was armed with a spear as thick as a
weaver's beam. Benaiah wrenched the spear from the Egyptian's
hand and killed him with it. Deeds like these made Benaiah as
famous as the three mightiest warriors. (1 Chronicles 11:23–24)*

To forcibly take a spear out of a giant's hand and kill him with his
own weapon was not only a feat of strength, but also a point of
humiliation to the Egyptians. We have no indication of Benaiah's
size, but we get a strong indicator of what kind of man, soldier,
and warrior he was. With thirty men who were essentially David's Special Forces Unit and being given the position of captain
of the bodyguards, we know Benaiah was:

- Present
  A bodyguard is forced to be an in-the-moment, in-your-face kind of guy. With the dangerous circumstances David and his fighters often faced, staying alert and ready was a prerequisite.

- Protective
  Most of Benaiah's many battles would have been fighting to protect his king and his fellow soldiers. Living in a constant state of a protective posture would have been a normal and natural mode for him.

- Proactive
  From the few sentences about him and the incredible company he was in, Benaiah was a go-get-'em, get-it-done guy. If you chase a lion into a pit to kill it, you aren't the kind of man to wait around on others to act. We can assume when David needed something taken care of, Benaiah was a primary go-to for the king.

One final passage says a great deal about our man of the day with just a few words:

The third army commander, for the third month, was Benaiah son of Jehoiada the priest. He was chief and there were 24,000 men in his division. This was the Benaiah who was a mighty warrior among the Thirty and was over the Thirty. (1 Chronicles 27:5–6 NIV)

The ways I have seen God be proactive in my life are:

_____

_____

_____

_____

_____

_____

My "chasing a lion into a pit on a snowy day" moment with God would be when:

_____

_____

_____

_____

_____

_____

_____

"Heavenly Father, thank You that You were proactive to pursue me, and for giving examples like Benaiah, who weren't the major players in the story, but You used them to support and serve Your leaders and Your purposes. Help me to be present, protective, and proactive for the sake of those You have placed in my life, both to lead and to serve. In Jesus' name, amen."

MEMORY VERSE

JESUS SAID, "NO PROCRASTINATION.
NO BACKWARD LOOKS.
YOU CAN'T PUT GOD'S KINGDOM
OFF TILL TOMORROW.
SEIZE THE DAY."
- LUKE 9:62 MSG -

THE WORLD IS CHANGED
BY THOSE WHO
SHOW UP,
SPEAK UP,
AND STAND UP.

THE world IS THE PIT.
THE lion IS YOUR BATTLE.
YOU ARE Benaiah.
Today IS YOUR SNOWY DAY.

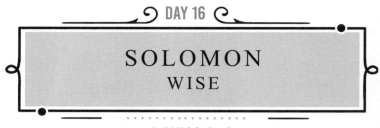

SOLOMON
WISE

1 KINGS 2–3

On his deathbed, King David handed his throne and rule over to his son. David's final charge to Solomon should be the final words of any father who follows Christ. In 1 Kings 2, he told him to take courage, be a man, and follow God and all His laws so he too could be successful in everything he does, everywhere he goes, wherever he rules. David encouraged his son that God would most certainly be faithful to His part of the covenant if Solomon would simply obey.

The new king honored his father, loved God, and followed His ways. The exchange between Solomon and God in and through a dream recorded in 1 Kings 3 is one of the most fascinating accounts in the Bible. The Lord appeared to him in a dream and said, "What do you want? Ask, and I will give it to you!" After recognizing God's faithfulness and love to his family, Solomon humbled himself and became completely transparent to his Heavenly Father.

"Now, O Lord my God, you have made me king instead of my father, David, but I am like a little child who doesn't know his way around. And here I am in the midst of your own chosen people, a

nation so great and numerous they cannot be counted! Give me an understanding heart so that I can govern your people well and know the difference between right and wrong. For who by himself is able to govern this great people of yours?" (1 Kings 3:7–9)

Taking the history of Israel's many leaders into account and their constant pattern of selfishness and poor decisions, God was overjoyed that Solomon would essentially follow the "greatest commandment," long before Jesus would share that truth, by putting God and the people before himself. He granted Solomon supernatural wisdom while also giving him vast wealth and a long life.

The story that follows proved beyond any doubt to the people that God had indeed placed His wisdom into the new king. Two prostitutes were granted access to Solomon to settle a dispute. Both women had recently given birth in the same house. One child had died, and now both mothers claimed the living child to be hers. After clarifying the details, without hesitation, Solomon asked for a sword. Playing out a bluff, he said he was going to cut the child in two and give each mother one-half of the body. Exactly what the king believed would happen did happen.

Then the woman who was the real mother of the living child, and who loved him very much, cried out, "Oh no, my lord! Give her the child—please do not kill him!" But the other woman said, "All right, he will be neither yours nor mine; divide him between us!" Then the king said, "Do not kill the child, but give him to the woman who wants him to live, for she is his mother!" When all Israel heard the king's decision, the people were in awe of the king, for they saw the wisdom God had given him for rendering justice. (1 Kings 3:26–28)

As a leader who loved God, life, and his people, Solomon had no intention of harming the child. But he knew the real mother's instincts and love would be sacrificial and create a horrified reaction. At the same time, the mother making the false claim showed her true colors. This split-second answer from Solomon sealed his new reputation and spread throughout the land. As we read Solomon's decisions throughout his life, we get a glimpse of the vast wisdom and knowledge of God.

A time I experienced God giving me wisdom for my life was:

_____

_____

_____

_____

_____

A time I experienced God giving me wisdom to benefit others was:

_____

_____

_____

_____

_____

"Heavenly Father, thank You that You are the sole Source of true wisdom, knowledge, and understanding. As Creator and Father, I can come to You for anything I need, and Your answers will be true and right. I ask that daily You grant me the wisdom I need to navigate life, love, and service to You and others. In Jesus' name, amen."

MEMORY VERSE

*IF YOU NEED WISDOM,
ASK OUR GENEROUS GOD,
AND HE WILL GIVE IT TO YOU.*

- JAMES 1:5 -

KNOWLEDGE CAN BE LEARNED ONE PAGE AT A TIME,
BUT WISDOM IS EARNED ONE DAY AT A TIME.

THE
CLOSER YOU GET
to *God,*
the deeper you go in
His Word,
the greater the
WISDOM
you will find.

ELIJAH
RECEPTIVE

1 KINGS 18–19

Elijah proved time and again that he was fully reliant on God. His level of obedience was amazing, and his receptivity to God's voice is one of the clearest channels we see in Scripture. The most public miracle God performed using Elijah was the standoff at Mount Carmel with the four hundred and fifty prophets of Baal with the entire nation of Israel watching. Elijah had two bulls brought to the altar, laid on top of wood, and had the prophets choose one. He challenged them to a contest to see whose God would rain fire down on the altar and burn up the sacrifice. Since he created the challenge, he invited the visiting team to go first.

The prophets of Baal spent all day dancing, chanting, shouting, and even cutting themselves to shed blood, but by evening nothing had happened. Now it was Elijah and God's turn. Knowing God would respond, Elijah piled up stones and added more wood, but then dug a trench around the altar and soaked the entire structure three times!

At the usual time for offering the evening sacrifice, Elijah the prophet walked up to the altar and prayed, "O LORD, God of Abraham, Isaac, and Jacob, prove today that you are God in Is-

rael and that I am your servant. Prove that I have done all this at your command. O LORD, answer me! Answer me so these people will know that you, O LORD, are God and that you have brought them back to yourself." Immediately the fire of the LORD flashed down from heaven and burned up the young bull, the wood, the stones, and the dust. It even licked up all the water in the trench! And when all the people saw it, they fell face down on the ground and cried out, "The LORD—he is God! Yes, the LORD is God!" (1 Kings 18:36–39)

One of the most powerful and inspiring events to speak to us in our own faith journey between Elijah and God is recorded in 1 Kings 19. When Jezebel sought revenge for the humiliation and destruction of the prophets of Baal, she threatened Elijah's life. Taking the warning seriously, God's prophet promptly left for Mount Sinai. The trip on foot took forty days and nights. Once he arrived at the mountain, Elijah found a cave to hide in.

Reminiscent of so many conversations between God and man, the Heavenly Father started with a question, knowing full well the answer. As the ultimate Parent, He knows what His child is doing and thinking, but asks to get a candid response. "What are you doing here, Elijah?" (v.9).

Elijah reminds God of the dire circumstances, informing the Creator that he has served him faithfully and now he is the only prophet left alive and they are after him too.

"Go out and stand before me on the mountain," the LORD told him. And as Elijah stood there, the LORD passed by, and a mighty windstorm hit the mountain. It was such a terrible blast that the rocks were torn loose, but the LORD was not in the wind. After the wind there was an earthquake, but the LORD was not in the earthquake. And after the earthquake there was a fire, but the LORD was not in the fire. And after the fire there was the sound of a gentle whisper. (1 Kings 19:11–12)

When we are praying for God to speak to us and work in our lives, we love and prefer the big write-it-in-the-sky moments. We want Him to speak big so we don't miss anything and have no choice but to know He has moved on our behalf.

We prefer the *remarkable*, while God prefers the *relationship*. We want to see a wind, fire, or earthquake as clear signs of His work when God just wants to speak with us.

The world has always been and will always be very loud, but God's voice can and will always be heard above the noise.

Elijah knew God's voice well because of the many times He had placed all his faith, belief, and trust in Him. He was unmoved in the wind, earthquake, and fire, but responded to the whisper of God: "When Elijah heard it, he wrapped his face in his cloak and went out and stood at the entrance of the cave" (1 Kings 19:13).

The time I know I heard God whisper to me above the noise of the world and other voices was:

_____

_____

_____

_____

_____

_____

Right now, amid the craziness of what is going on around me, I need to hear God speak to me regarding:

_____

_____

_____

_____

_____

_____

"Heavenly Father, I have been through so many of life's windstorms, earthquakes, and fires in my life. Thank You for the many times You have protected me, sustained me, and led me through those. Please help me to be more and more receptive to Your Word and Your whisper. In Jesus' name, amen."

MEMORY VERSE

AND AFTER THE FIRE THERE
WAS THE SOUND OF A GENTLE WHISPER.

- 1 KINGS 19:12 -

**LEADERS CAN HEAR CLEARLY IN THE STORM,
HOLD STEADY ON SHAKY GROUND,
AND WALK THROUGH THE FIRE.**

STAND STRONG
in the storm
& listen for
God's whisper.

HEZEKIAH
CONSISTENT

2 KINGS 18—20

Hezekiah's story begins in 2 Kings 18, where we are told right away that starting his reign at twenty-five years old, Hezekiah did what was pleasing in the Lord's sight, just like his ancestor David. He removed idols and altars that had anything to do with other gods. He obeyed God's commands. God was with him, and he was successful in everything he did. What an amazing record of legacy.

The king of Assyria sent a long threatening and blasphemous letter to King Hezekiah. The letter mocked Hezekiah and God, attempting to incite the people against the king. He worked hard in his document to cast doubt, poke fun, and insult, all the while bragging of his great power and domination of other nations. Here is an excerpt:

"Don't listen to Hezekiah when he tries to mislead you by saying, 'The LORD will rescue us!' Have the gods of any other nations ever saved their people from the king of Assyria? What happened to the gods of Hamath and Arpad? And what about the gods of Sepharvaim, Hena, and Ivvah? Did any god rescue Samaria from my power? What god of any nation has ever been able to

save its people from my power? So what makes you think that the LORD can rescue Jerusalem from me?" (2 Kings 18:32–35)

The nation stood strong and trusted their God and their king.

But the people were silent and did not utter a word because Hezekiah had commanded them, "Do not answer him." (2 Kings 18:36)

Following the delivery of the threat, Hezekiah didn't assemble his military generals or express fear or concern to his counsel. He went straight to the Temple, spread the letter out before God, and prayed. After offering recognition and worship to the Lord, he interceded for the nation.

"Now, O LORD our God, rescue us… then all the kingdoms of the earth will know that you alone, O LORD, are God." (2 Kings 19:19)

The prophet Isaiah then came to deliver a message from God that no army would enter Jerusalem, for the Lord Himself would protect them.

That night the angel of the LORD went out to the Assyrian camp and killed 185,000 Assyrian soldiers. When the surviving Assyrians woke up the next morning, they found corpses everywhere. Then King Sennacherib of Assyria broke camp and returned to his own land. (2 Kings 19:35–36)

That was how Hezekiah handled the external threat of war, but then an internal threat came. The king became deathly ill, and Isaiah came to inform him that he needed to prepare his affairs because he would die. Once again, Hezekiah turned immediately to his faith and trust in God.

When Hezekiah heard this, he turned his face to the wall and prayed to the Lord, "Remember, O LORD, how I have always been faithful to you and have served you single-mindedly, always doing what pleases you." Then he broke down and wept bitterly. (2 Kings 20:2–3)

Before Isaiah could leave the palace, God sent a new message. God heard Hezekiah's words and saw his tears. He would be healed and live another fifteen years. The text here appears to indicate his days were up, but God decided to give him more years to answer his prayer. Yet another clear sign that God has always been and still is pursuing a relationship with His people. He listens and He answers.

What tends to be your first response when external or internal threats come into your life?

_____

_____

_____

_____

_____

_____

As a leader in any setting, when threats arise, where and how do you tend to lead others?

_____

_____

_____

_____

_____

_____

"Heavenly Father, thank You for examples of national leaders who sought Your help and counsel above any other possible answers. Help me in any and all circumstances where I lead to take this challenge and come to You—privately and publicly. In Jesus' name, amen."

MEMORY VERSE

You alone are God of all the kingdoms of the earth. You alone created the heavens and the earth. Bend down, O Lord, and listen! Open your eyes, O Lord, and see!

- 2 Kings 19:15 -

**WHEN A THREAT ARRIVES,
A LEADER THRIVES.**

GOD
HEARS PRAYERS,

SEES TEARS,
and touches
hearts.

JOSIAH
COURAGEOUS

2 KINGS 22–23

In 2 Kings 22, we read that Josiah became king at eight years old and ruled in Jerusalem for thirty-one years. When he had been king for eighteen years, he sent two of his staff to arrange for repairs to the Temple.

To everyone's surprise, while there they found the Book of the Law of their ancestors. When the scroll was returned to Jerusalem and read to the king, he compared its words to their actions. Josiah quickly understood that because of their ignorance of what God wanted, they were in deep trouble. Expressing his reverence and belief, his response of repentance was revolutionary to his nation.

"Go to the Temple and speak to the LORD for me and for the people and for all Judah. Inquire about the words written in this scroll that has been found. For the LORD's great anger is burning against us because our ancestors have not obeyed the words in this scroll. We have not been doing everything it says we must do." (2 Kings 22:13)

Because God saw Josiah's sorrowful response to the Law, He

promised to withhold judgment. Josiah responded by gathering all the religious leaders along with all the people of Judah and Jerusalem. He took on the responsibility of having the people hear the Word of God from his own lips. He didn't delegate the work to the priests or prophets. He read the entire Book of the Law himself out loud publicly to everyone. He then renewed the covenant with God and encouraged the nation to follow His leadership. Before all the people, he pledged to obey God's commands, laws, and decrees.

But Josiah was not done yet. He set up his offense in front of everyone. Now it was time for his defense to take the field. He went through the countryside, having everything connected to idols removed and burned. Anything, anyone, anywhere that was connected to any idol or altar to worship of something other than God was dismantled and destroyed. He executed pagan priests while putting a stop to child sacrifice. Josiah literally and spiritually cleaned house! When he had overseen the destruction of all idols and altars, he returned home to Jerusalem and reinstated Passover for the first time in many years.

Take a close look at these two verses and consider the weight of these words to describe *any* man, much less the king of any nation in history.

He did what was pleasing in the LORD's sight and followed the example of his ancestor David. He did not turn away from doing what was right. (2 Kings 22:2)

Never before had there been a king like Josiah, who turned to the LORD with all his heart and soul and strength, obeying all the laws of Moses. And there has never been a king like him since. (2 Kings 23:25)

- Josiah cared more about what God thought than anyone else.

  Think about the political, cultural, and religious pressure Josiah had to ignore to obey God. We must not minimize these aspects or think them to be any less in that day. He knew his position of authority had been given to get the nation right with God. His relationship with Him was his identity, not his crown. He owned his title; his title didn't own him.

- Josiah stayed on course with God's will, not distracted by the world's ways.

  In any culture throughout history, sin has always existed. As a king, the amount of distractions to sin only increased, as he had anything he wanted with a word. Josiah put his hand to the plow for God's Kingdom and never looked to the right, the left, or behind him, just as Jesus stated we all must do.

- Josiah loved the Lord with all his heart, soul, and strength in words and actions.

  We first find this phrase spoken by Moses to the people in Deuteronomy 6:5. Later Jesus spoke these words to present the greatest commandment. This is the culmination of the Bible from Josiah to Jesus, as well as to us today, to love the Lord with all our hearts, souls, minds, and strength.

The most profound change I had to make in my life since I came to Christ was:

_____

_____

_____

_____

_____

_____

One thing I know I still need to do to "clean house" spiritually is:

_____

_____

_____

_____

_____

_____

"Heavenly Father, help me to care more about what You think than anyone else in my life; to stay on course with Your will, not distracted by the world's ways; and to love You with all my heart, soul, and strength in my words and in my actions. In Jesus' name, amen."

MEMORY VERSE

Write your name in the blank to personalize and memorize this adaptation of today's verse:

_____

DID WHAT WAS PLEASING IN THE LORD'S SIGHT AND ...
HE DID NOT TURN AWAY FROM DOING WHAT WAS RIGHT.

- 2 KINGS 22:2 -

**LEADERS SACRIFICE
TO MAKE THE HARD CALLS
FOR THE BEST OF EVERYONE ELSE,
EVEN IF THEY MUST STAND ALONE.**

Only through Christ CAN WE DO *what is right* AND BE PLEASING IN *God's sight.*

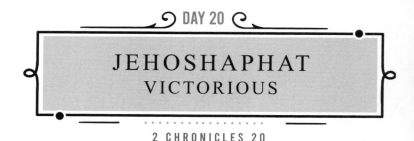

JEHOSHAPHAT
VICTORIOUS

2 CHRONICLES 20

In the days when Jehoshaphat was king of Judah, word came to him that the Moabites, Ammonites, and Meunites had declared war on his nation. They were gathered together as a massive fighting force and marching toward him.

While fear struck him, his faith in God was his go-to response. He immediately began to pray, and ordered the people to fast and to gather in Jerusalem to publicly and corporately seek God.

When the people had arrived, he stood in the Temple courtyard and prayed aloud. After the king recognized God's power and His place in their lives, while also connecting their history with the nation, he confessed their humility and helplessness before such a vast enemy and begged for God's intervention.

Following Jehoshaphat's prayer, God's Spirit spoke through one of the Levites. The word began as so many others in Scripture: "Do not be afraid! Don't be discouraged!" Then very strange yet specific instructions came next.

"Tomorrow, march out against them. You will find them coming

*up through the ascent of Ziz at the end of the valley that opens
into the wilderness of Jeruel. But you will not even need to fight.
Take your positions; then stand still and watch the LORD's victory. He is with you, O people of Judah and Jerusalem. Do not
be afraid or discouraged. Go out against them tomorrow, for
the LORD is with you!" (2 Chronicles 20:16–17)*

Let's review, shall we? March out against the mass force of the
three enemy armies. Take your battle positions as if you are going to fight. Then just stand still and watch. Again, as we see so
many times in Scripture, the command to not be afraid or discouraged is repeated.

In the history of wars and battles, we see two clear responses to
an approaching invasion: attack or retreat, advance or run. As
God so often has done throughout history, He offered a different
plan than the usual human response: advance, wait, and watch.

The next morning, without question and believing God, they did
exactly what He instructed. But as they began to march toward
the battlefield, they added one element: they worshiped as they
marched toward the battle. The Scripture states that as soon as the
people began to advance and worship, God caused the armies to
begin fighting themselves. Much like we saw in Gideon's story.

Try to put yourself in the place of a Jewish warrior. As you come
over the hill at the lookout point, knowing the armies are gathered below, all you see are dead bodies with no sign of who or

what had taken them all out.

Then all the men returned to Jerusalem, with Jehoshaphat lead-ing them, overjoyed that the LORD had given them victory over their enemies. They marched into Jerusalem to the music of harps, lyres, and trumpets, and they proceeded to the Temple of the LORD. When all the surrounding kingdoms heard that the LORD himself had fought against the enemies of Israel, the fear of God came over them. So Jehoshaphat's kingdom was at peace, for his God had given him rest on every side. (2 Chronicles 20:27–30)

God was able to give King Jehoshaphat and the nation total vic-tory because:

- He went to God first.
- He obeyed God.
- He saw God's victory.
- He listened to God.
- He worshiped God.
- He experienced God's peace.

This pattern appears to be quite simple, but we can so often get distracted and sidetracked at any point. A major element in this story that is also a powerful and effective truth for us all is found in verse 15: "For the battle is not yours, but God's."

In our daily walk with Christ, we must listen and discern which battles are God's so we can know to not fight, but to take our positions, stand still, and watch His victory.

A battle I knew I had to wait on the Lord and allow Him to fight for me was:

_____

_____

_____

_____

_____

_____

An impending battle I know is approaching where I need God's help is:

_____

_____

_____

_____

_____

_____

"Heavenly Father, thank You that You involve us when the battle is actually Yours. To simply worship, wait, and watch is so hard for us to do as sinful men. Help me to learn from this truth and apply it when You speak. In Jesus' name, amen."

MEMORY VERSE

Write your name in the blank to personalize and memorize this adaptation of today's verse:

BUT YOU WILL NOT EVEN NEED TO FIGHT.
TAKE YOUR POSITIONS;
THEN STAND STILL AND WATCH THE LORD'S VICTORY.
HE IS WITH YOU,

_____

DO NOT BE AFRAID OR DISCOURAGED ...
FOR THE LORD IS WITH YOU!"
- 2 CHRONICLES 20:17, ADAPTED -

**LEADERS KNOW WHEN TO FIGHT,
WHEN TO TAKE POSITION AND BE READY,
AND WHEN TO SIMPLY WATCH AND WAIT.**

WORSHIP
God's ways.

WAIT
on God's word.

WATCH
for God's will.

NEHEMIAH
PROBLEM SOLVER

NEHEMIAH 1—6

Nehemiah was King Artaxerxes' cupbearer at the fortress of Susa when a group of men led by his brother came to meet with him. When they informed Nehemiah that the walls of Jerusalem were torn down and the gates had been burned, he wept and mourned. But then he began to pray and fast for God's help.

When Artaxerxes saw Nehemiah's countenance was uncharacteristically sad, he asked his cupbearer what was troubling him. Being completely honest with the king about the news regarding Jerusalem, Nehemiah requested time away along with letters granting permission for resources to go and "rebuild the city."

The obvious care and respect that King Artaxerxes had for Nehemiah was proven as he granted everything his cupbearer asked. That immediate agreement and provision tells us a great deal about the high level of integrity, trust, and respect the king had for him. Adding more to his credit, Nehemiah knew right away that God had answered his prayers by granting the king's favor.

As Nehemiah began to devise a plan and gather his people to rebuild the wall, opposition quickly raised its head. Yet, the next chapters in the book state in great detail who worked on what area. Under his leadership, progress came quickly while the enemy's threats escalated.

Then as I looked over the situation, I called together the nobles and the rest of the people and said to them, "Don't be afraid of the enemy! Remember the LORD, who is great and glorious, and fight for your brothers, your sons, your daughters, your wives, and your homes!" When our enemies heard that we knew of their plans and that God had frustrated them, we all returned to our work on the wall. ... The laborers carried on their work with one hand supporting their load and one hand holding a weapon. All the builders had a sword belted to their side. ... We worked early and late, from sunrise to sunset. And half the men were always on guard. ... During this time, none of us—not I, nor my relatives, nor my servants, nor the guards who were with me—ever took off our clothes. We carried our weapons with us at all times, even when we went for water. (Nehemiah 4:14–15, 17, 21, 23)

As men who follow Christ, we know we have a *work to do in this world* between now and Heaven. We also know we need God's *weapons to fight the spiritual battle* we face every day in our world. Living in the Kingdom of God while walking in the kingdom of darkness in this culture demands a powerful offense coupled with a strong defense to succeed. Like Nehemiah encouraged the people, we have to do our work with one hand and wield a weapon in the other to, as Paul stated in Ephesians 6:10, "be strong in the Lord and in his mighty power."

Nehemiah 6 records that fifty-two days after Nehemiah had begun, the wall was finished. When the news got out that the building was completed, all those who had opposed God's leader and His people were scared and humiliated because everyone saw what God had done for His people.

As men, we take on projects all the time as a part of our career, home, church, or community. We understand what it takes to gather and motivate people, how to deal with opposition, and also how to invite God to lead us as we lead.

Let's look at some key qualities of Nehemiah that helped him succeed in the eyes of God, the people, and even his enemies.

As external qualities, Nehemiah:	As internal qualities, Nehemiah was:
Cast the vision	Unashamedly bold
Rallied the people	Unwavering in honesty
Focused on the goal	Unmoved in faith

My personal faith and relationship with Christ have most helped me with problem-solving by:

_____

_____

_____

_____

_____

_____

My strongest quality I have seen God use in my life to add value to people and projects is:

_____

_____

_____

_____

_____

_____

"Heavenly Father, so much of our lives is spent building and rebuilding many things with other people. Give me wisdom and help me to always be a part of the solution and not add to the problem. Give me eyes and ears to know who You want me to help, when You want me to help, and how I can best help to glorify You and serve others. In Jesus' name, amen."

MEMORY VERSE

TODAY IS HOLY TO OUR LORD, SO DON'T BE SAD. THE JOY THAT THE LORD GIVES YOU WILL MAKE YOU STRONG."

- NEHEMIAH 8:10 GNT -

LEADERS CAN RUN
A GREAT OFFENSE,
WHILE SHUTTING DOWN OPPOSITION
WITH A STRONG DEFENSE.

KEEP
YOUR WORK
IN ONE HAND TO
glorify God
AND YOUR WEAPON
IN THE OTHER TO
DEFEAT
THE ENEMY.

MORDECAI
INSIGHT

ESTHER 1—8

In the book of Esther, Xerxes was king as the son and successor of Darius. Esther and Mordecai were cousins, but when her parents died, Mordecai brought her into his household to raise her like an adopted daughter. Their family was originally from Judah and had been exiled to Babylon from Jerusalem by Nebuchadnezzar. The Bible rarely describes anyone's physical appearance, so when that is included in the text, we have to pay attention. Esther 2 calls her beautiful, lovely, and young.

When the most beautiful young ladies were brought before Xerxes to search for a replacement of the queen, of course, Esther was a high draft pick. But she never mentioned that she was Jewish. Being a protective and involved adopted dad, Mordecai went by the palace to try to check on Esther. When she was finally brought before the king, he was taken with her and immediately decided she was the new queen.

From hanging out near the palace and trying to gather intel on Esther, Mordecai discovered an assassination plot. He got the news to Esther, who then brought the report before the king. Mordecai's proactive work saved the king.

But as in any good story, an evil villain with a secret agenda and a huge ego is introduced. A noble named Haman worked his way up the food chain and was promoted to second-in-command. The protocol demanded that when Haman passed by, people were required to bow. Mordecai, being a man of wisdom and insight, sensed the new official wasn't worthy of his position, so he refused to bow or respect his authority.

Enraged, Haman decided he would more than do away with Mordecai. Because he had found out Mordecai was a Jew, he determined to have *all* Jews eliminated. (Sounds sadly familiar, doesn't it?) Haman went to the king and told him of a "certain race of people" who kept themselves separate and ignored his laws. He recommended the king issue an official order to have every man, woman, and child destroyed. The king trusted Haman's word and agreed.

Esther and Mordecai managed to get messages to one another so she could know about the plot to kill her people. Mordecai's famous line to Esther in his final plea was, "Who knows if perhaps you were made queen for just such a time as this?" (4:14). Esther knew she could be put to death if she tried to go before the king when she had not been summoned. But she sent word to Mordecai for the people to fast and pray, and determined to risk her life for her people.

As Esther was working a brilliant plan to invite the king and Haman to two days of private banquets, Haman saw Mordecai, who once again would not bow, and vowed to get rid of him. At the suggestion of his wife and friends, he set up a seventy-five-foot pole to impale Mordecai. Meanwhile, God was at work.

One night as the king was reading his personal history, he was reminded of Mordecai's uncovering of the assassination plot. When Haman showed up to request permission to impale Mordecai, the king instead asked his advice on how to honor a man. Haman arrogantly assumed the king was referring to him and offered an elaborate display of celebration. The king loved the idea and ordered Haman to take care of this for *Mordecai.*

Humiliated, Haman went to the second day of Esther's banquet. There, when the king asked Esther what this event was really all about, she divulged Haman's plot. Infuriated, the king ordered Haman to be impaled on the very pole he had erected for Mordecai. Esther then convinced the king to stop the execution of her people.

King Xerxes imposed a tribute throughout his empire, even to the distant coastlands. His great achievements and the full account of the greatness of Mordecai, whom the king had promoted, are recorded in The Book of the History of the Kings of Media and Persia. Mordecai the Jew became the prime minister, with authority next to that of King Xerxes himself. He was very great among the Jews, who held him in high esteem, because he continued to work for the good of his people and to speak up for the welfare of all their descendants. (Esther 10)

A circumstance where I knew God gave me special insight was:

_____

_____

_____

_____

_____

_____

A circumstance where I saw God vindicate me when someone intended harm was:

_____

_____

_____

_____

_____

_____

"Heavenly Father, thank You for Your faithfulness, watch-care, and knowing I can trust You to take care of me, even when I can't discern others' motives. Give boldness and the insight to do the right thing, no matter the cost. I know You will see my obedience and honor my choices to please You. In Jesus' name, amen."

MEMORY VERSE

AND WHO KNOWS BUT THAT YOU HAVE COME TO YOUR POSITION FOR SUCH A TIME AS THIS?"

- ESTHER 4:14 NIV, ADAPTED -

LEADERS MAKE THE HARD CALL TO DO THE RIGHT THING, EVEN IN THE FACE OF PERSONAL RISK.

God HAS PLACED *who you are,* WHERE YOU ARE, *for what He needs,* WHEN THE TIME IS RIGHT *to fulfill His* *purposes* AND HIS PLAN.

DAY 23

JOB
PERSEVERANCE

JOB 1–2, 38–42

One of the most disturbing yet challenging stories in Scripture is that of Job. The very first verse in his book states he is "blameless—a man of complete integrity" who "feared God and stayed away from evil" (1:1). But he appeared to get unknowingly caught up in some sort of supernatural battle between God and Satan. To make matters worse, we are never told that Job knew what was being said about him in the heavenly realm. He was just left to deal with what was brought upon him in the physical world. But that is likely one of the main purposes for this story being in the Bible.

When God stated the truth about Job, Satan came back at Him, "Well, of course he follows you! You protect him and prosper him. Look at how rich he is. But if you take everything away, he will surely curse you." God agreed to allow Job to be tested, with the only boundary being Satan could not kill him! So, Satan immediately went to work destroying all of Job's livelihood and then his entire family. His wife was all he had left, and Satan even had plans for her. Yet Job's response was quite amazing.

"The LORD gave me what I had, and the LORD has taken it

away. Praise the name of the LORD!" In all of this, Job did not sin by blaming God. (Job 1:21–22)

Then the same exact scene occurred between God and Satan again. And God again allowed for Job to be tested. This time he was covered with painful, ugly boils from head to toe. At this point, his wife chimed in, "Are you still trying to maintain your integrity? Curse God and die" (2:9). Yet again, Job did not sin.

As Job was sitting outside, three of his friends came to visit with their advice, opinions, and judgment. They had no clue that God was right in the middle of Job's circumstance. Even though they were men of knowledge and wisdom, the problem was not in what they knew, but what they didn't know. The back-and-forth of trying to "fix" Job went on for many chapters with long, insensitive, and sometimes cruel monologues.

The three types of friends that emerge in a crisis are: those who don't show up, those who show up but make it about them, and then those who show up and keep it about you. Job also offers us principles for ministry, such as when someone is hurting, they need:

- Grace, not Law
- Love, not a solution
- A relational interaction, not a religious intervention
- Someone to sit in silence and support
- Someone to express empathy, not sympathy

In Job 38, God spoke and did not stop until the end of chapter 41, offering some of the most compelling and humbling words in the Bible, because they are direct quotes from God. By chapter 42, Job had a revelation, which is likely the very point of all God had done.

I had only heard about you before, but now I have seen you with my own eyes. (v.5)

In the end, instead of getting his questions answered, Job got God Himself. Instead of his friends' secondhand info about God, he received firsthand experience with God. He had an eternal experience arise out of a horrific temporary state, after having required that God come and give reason for His judgment. But God didn't come with answers but His own questions, because He will never be put on the defense.

God never mentioned Job's sins. His friends did. God never mentioned Job's suffering. Satan did. But in the end, Job was exonerated as not the worst of men, but the best.

So the LORD blessed Job in the second half of his life even more than in the beginning. ... Job lived 140 years after that, living to see four generations of his children and grandchildren. Then he died, an old man who had lived a long, full life. (Job 42:12, 16–17)

The greatest spiritual testing I have experienced was:

_____

_____

_____

_____

_____

_____

God has used that difficult season of my life by/ to:

_____

_____

_____

_____

_____

_____

_____

"Heavenly Father, I know You don't test us to see what we are made of, because You already know. You show us so that we can see. Help me to trust You when the tests come, when tragedy strikes. Help me to view Job's story as encouragement and inspiration to seek You in the midst of trials. In Jesus' name, amen."

MEMORY VERSE

*I HAD ONLY HEARD ABOUT YOU BEFORE,
BUT NOW I HAVE SEEN YOU WITH MY OWN EYES.*

- JOB 42:5 -

LEADERS DON'T OFFER EXCUSES,
BUT OFFER AN EXAMPLE
BY TAKING PERSONAL RESPONSIBILITY
FOR THEIR OWN DECISIONS AND ACTIONS.

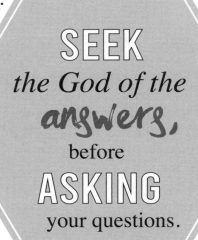

SEEK
the God of the
answers,
before
ASKING
your questions.

DANIEL
UNCOMPROMISING

DANIEL 1–2, 6

In Daniel 1, after King Nebuchadnezzar had invaded Jerusalem and taken captives back to Babylon, he ordered some of the young men of nobility who were "strong, healthy, and good-looking" be brought into the palace. He wanted to train them over three years for royal service. Daniel, along with Shadrach, Meshach, and Abednego, were chosen, which immediately tells us a lot about these guys.

The first challenge came when Daniel found out they would be fed a Babylonian diet of rich foods with wine. Daniel's disagreement is assumed to have been because certain foods were against Jewish Law and may have been associated with idols and idol worship. So he offered a ten-day test to the chief of staff, requesting that he and his three friends eat only vegetables and water. Understanding diet today, coupled with God's blessing, the result was no surprise. The four young Jewish men were healthier and better nourished than the others. As a result, they were allowed to continue their own diet.

Following Daniel's legendary royal dream interpretation that God provided, he was promoted to a high position and requested his buddies Shadrach, Meshach, and Abednego receive favor as well.

Meanwhile, to no surprise, as Daniel kept getting promotions and favor, the other officials were ready to get rid of him. (Much like the Pharisees' response to Jesus.) They decided that Daniel's faith was the best way to get him. By now Nebuchadnezzar was gone and Darius was on the throne. They convinced him to create a new law that everyone had to pray to the king; anyone caught praying to anyone or anything else would be thrown to the lions. (They had already seen that a fiery furnace didn't work.)

Daniel heard the law and not only kept praying three times a day, but he also threw open his windows toward Jerusalem so anyone could hear him! The tattletales quickly ran to the king. The scene that plays out is almost comical as they worked their manipulation. Though the king did not want to carry out the sentence on Daniel, with his power on the line, he relented and gave the order.

King Darius blessed Daniel with the hope that his God would save him and then spent the night fasting and abstaining from his usual indulgences.

Very early the next morning, the king got up and hurried out to the lions' den. When he got there, he called out in anguish, "Daniel, servant of the living God! Was your God, whom you serve so faithfully, able to rescue you from the lions?" Daniel answered, "Long live the king! My God sent his angel to shut the lions' mouths so that they would not hurt me, for I have been found innocent in his sight. And I have not wronged you, Your Majesty." The king was overjoyed and ordered that Daniel be lifted from the den. Not a scratch was found on him, for he had trusted in his God. (Daniel 6:19–23)

Every time a crisis came to Daniel and his three friends, they did not suddenly decide to become men of great faith. Their beliefs were an overflow of their everyday commitment to God. Anyone can run to Him in a 9-1-1 moment, but following God in the best of days allows for strength and favor for the worst of times.

My "lion's den" moment of faith came when:

_____

_____

_____

_____

_____

_____

The biggest opportunity I have had to publicly glorify God by my obedience to Him was:

_____

_____

_____

_____

_____

_____

"Heavenly Father, thank You for the many truths and principles gleaned from Daniel's story. Help me to store these events up in my heart so when my moments of crisis and trial come, I can be encouraged to put You first and follow You no matter what the culture states. In Jesus' name, amen."

MEMORY VERSE

Daniel 1:8 is a great verse to personalize and memorize to encourage you with any temptation. Write your name in the first blank and your struggle in the second blank.

BUT _____

WAS DETERMINED NOT TO DEFILE HIMSELF BY

_____

- DANIEL 1:8 -

THE TOUGHEST CALLS A LEADER MAKES IN PUBLIC OFTEN COME WITH THE GREATEST COST IN PRIVATE.

Following

GOD

in the best of days
allows for

STRENGTH

and favor

for the worst of times.

SHADRACH, MESHACH, AND ABEDNEGO
SYNERGY

DANIEL 1, 3

Yesterday in Daniel, we talked briefly about his three buddies who made up the vegetables-and-water-diet group from Daniel 1. The chief of staff had given them Babylonian names. Verse 7 explains, "Daniel was called Belteshazzar. Hananiah was called Shadrach. Mishael was called Meshach. Azariah was called Abednego."

God gave these four young men an unusual aptitude for understanding every aspect of literature and wisdom. ... When the training period ordered by the king was completed, the chief of staff brought all the young men to King Nebuchadnezzar. The king talked with them, and no one impressed him as much as Daniel, Hananiah, Mishael, and Azariah. So they entered the royal service. Whenever the king consulted them in any matter requiring wisdom and balanced judgment, he found them ten times more capable than any of the magicians and enchanters in his entire kingdom. (Daniel 1:17–20)

After Daniel had interpreted Nebuchadnezzar's dream, the king appointed him as ruler over the entire province of Babylonia. Being stationed in the king's court, Daniel placed his three friends in high positions as well.

When Nebuchadnezzar decided to set up a ninety-foot gold statue of himself to be worshiped, of course these three men of God refused to bow. Compelled to enforce his own mandate, the king decided to offer a second chance to Shadrach, Meshach, and Abednego to recant by threatening their lives with a blazing furnace.

Shadrach, Meshach, and Abednego replied, "O Nebuchadnezzar, we do not need to defend ourselves before you. If we are thrown into the blazing furnace, the God whom we serve is able to save us. He will rescue us from your power, Your Majesty. But even if he doesn't, we want to make it clear to you, Your Majesty, that we will never serve your gods or worship the gold statue you have set up." (Daniel 3:16–18)

In response to their defiance, the king commanded the furnace be stoked seven times hotter than normal. Not taking any chances, he had his strongest men tie the three friends up. When the men threw Shadrach, Meshach, and Abednego into the flames, the intense heat was so strong that it killed the king's men. But that's when things began to get really interesting.

Evidently Nebuchadnezzar was watching from some high, safe vantage point, looking down into the flames. Peering into the furnace, he soon realized that not only were the three men not being burned up, but a fourth man was inside with them too. The king also saw that they were still fully clothed and their restraints were gone. The language used in the text allows for the miraculous reality that Jesus was actually the fourth man with them.

King Nebuchadnezzar called down into the fire for the men to come out. The three friends walked out unharmed. The fourth man was never mentioned again. The fact that they walked out not even smelling of smoke offers an amazing connection to our own salvation in escaping the fires of Hell, also because of Jesus' presence in our lives. Yet again, a Babylonian king was forced to recognize the God of the Jews.

Then Nebuchadnezzar said, "Praise to the God of Shadrach, Meshach, and Abednego! He sent his angel to rescue his servants who trusted in him. They defied the king's command and were willing to die rather than serve or worship any god except their own God. Therefore, I make this decree: If any people, whatever their race or nation or language, speak a word against the God of Shadrach, Meshach, and Abednego, they will be torn limb from limb, and their houses will be turned into heaps of rubble. There is no other god who can rescue like this!" (Daniel 3:28–29)

The king then promoted Shadrach, Meshach, and Abednego to even higher positions than Daniel had placed them. Can you imagine when he was reunited with his three friends, the joy, laughter, celebration, and worship they must have expressed?

Who are the men in your life with whom you have "walked through the fire"? The men who have your back spiritually as well as physically?

_____

_____

_____

_____

_____

_____

Who are the men whose lives you are pouring into, just like Daniel did for his three friends?

_____

_____

_____

_____

_____

_____

"Heavenly Father, thank You for my 'fire friends' who I can trust for help in any crisis. Thank You that, ultimately, You are the God about whom even pagan kings have to say, 'There is no other god who can rescue like this!' Help me to be the kind of man in Your Kingdom who can pour into and bless other men. In Jesus' name, amen."

MEMORY VERSE

Write your name in the blank to personalize and memorize this adaptation of today's verse:

_____

WAS WILLING TO DIE RATHER THAN SERVE OR WORSHIP ANY GOD EXCEPT [HIS] OWN GOD.

- DANIEL 3:28, ADAPTED -

**LEADERS CREATE SYNERGY
WHERE TEAMWORK IS GREATER AND STRONGER
THAN INDIVIDUAL EFFORTS.**

A person standing *alone* ━CAN BE━

attacked and defeated,

BUT TWO CAN STAND

stand back-to-back and

conquer.

THREE ARE EVEN BETTER,
*for a triple-braided cord
is not easily broken.*

ECCLESIASTES 4:12

ZECHARIAH
TEACHABLE

LUKE 1

In Luke 1, we are told that Zechariah and Elizabeth are both from families of priests. They had served God faithfully throughout their lives, even though He had not answered their primary prayer of being able to have children. In their culture, having a child was viewed as a direct blessing from God, with the number of children being a sign of how blessed. For this reason, being prominent priests but childless brought on criticism and ridicule. Living with religious and pious gossip was a constant thorn in their side. And the older they got, the more hopeless the couple became.

Twenty-four divisions of priests meant that Zechariah was on duty for one week, twice a year. The honor of being the designated priest to enter the Holy of Holies was the highest possible responsibility. Some served their entire lifetimes without having the privilege. Because the priests were equals, and there were always more men than responsibilities, dice were tossed to make the choice. Imagine Zechariah's joy and sense of redemption when he won. His once-in-a lifetime moment had finally arrived.

As the large crowd gathered outside, prayerful and humble, Zechariah made his way inside. Suddenly, beside the altar, an angel appeared. And not just any angel, but Gabriel himself.

"Don't be afraid, Zechariah! God has heard your prayer. Your wife, Elizabeth, will give you a son, and you are to name him John. You will have great joy and gladness, and many will rejoice at his birth, for he will be great in the eyes of the Lord." (Luke 1:13–15)

Gabriel told Zechariah what the baby's calling would be and that the Messiah was also on the way. But the years of questions and doubts must have taken over in Zechariah's heart, because when he should have stayed silent, or simply agreed, the priest asked, "How can I be sure this will happen?"

When Mary was visited by Gabriel to tell her of Jesus, she asked, "How can this happen since I am a virgin?" But there's a difference between "How can this happen?" and "How can I be sure this will happen?" One is a question of logistics and the other of loyalty.

Gabriel sternly reminded Zechariah who he was questioning and then delivered the consequence: the priest would not be able to speak until his child was born. The one thing you would want to do as an elderly man who had prayed for a son your entire married life would be to tell anyone and everyone the great news! But because Zechariah questioned God's message, his own speech would be taken away. He would be shown the power of the spoken word—firsthand.

When Zechariah came out of the Holy of Holies, the other priests quickly realized something significant had taken place and he was mute. Following his week of service, Zechariah went home, and just as God said, Elizabeth became pregnant with John, conceived by natural method for supernatural purposes. Once the baby was born, the family was confused by Elizabeth's insistence on the child's name so they went to the mute father for an answer, literally for a sign.

He motioned for a writing tablet, and to everyone's surprise he wrote, "His name is John." Instantly Zechariah could speak again, and he began praising God. Awe fell upon the whole neighborhood, and the news of what had happened spread throughout the Judean hills. Everyone who heard about it reflected on these events and asked, "What will this child turn out to be?" For the hand of the Lord was surely upon him in a special way. (Luke 1:63–66)

Three principles we can learn from Zechariah's silent service are:

1. Serving God faithfully will bring blessing, but in His time, not ours.

2. God is at work on our behalf, even when we can't see, hear, or understand what He's doing.

3. When God speaks, the best choice is always to obey without question.

I was given a Zechariah consequence the time that I:

_____

_____

_____

_____

_____

_____

_____

God used that consequence in my life to show me:

_____

_____

_____

_____

_____

_____

_____

167

"Heavenly Father, when You speak to me, whether to answer my prayers or invite me into Your work, give me ears to hear and the faith to say yes without question or doubts. Zechariah's story also reminds me to keep praying because You will answer every prayer in Your time and in Your way. In Jesus' name, amen."

MEMORY VERSE

WE CAN SERVE GOD WITHOUT FEAR,
IN HOLINESS AND RIGHTEOUSNESS
FOR AS LONG AS WE LIVE.

- LUKE 1:74–75 -

A LEADER WAITS PATIENTLY FOR HIS MOMENT,
GUARDS HIS MOUTH, AND IS
FAITHFUL WITH HIS MESSAGE.

SERVING
GOD FAITHFULLY
WILL BRING
blessing,
BUT IN
His time,
NOT OURS.

JOSEPH
SELF-SACRIFICING

MATTHEW 1

In Christmas manger scenes, one figure tends to be overlooked and undervalued, and at times, he even seems to be invisible. In the story of the birth of Christ, told every year to millions, one prominent character is virtually ignored yet is absolutely crucial to the story. Throughout the Gospels, Jesus' relationship with His Heavenly Father was ever present, but He also had an earthly father—Joseph.

Imagine being chosen to raise God's only Son, knowing all the while, your child is not your "blood." If you have never really taken a serious look at Joseph, I have a feeling your respect for him is about to go way up.

First, his lineage, found in Luke 1:27, is important to know: "Joseph was of the family of David" (NLV). His fiancée, Mary, came to him claiming that an angel had appeared to her and that God had spiritually impregnated her with His Son. Oh, and by the way, this baby will be the Savior of the world. How many men would believe that story, no matter what era they lived in?

Matthew 1:19 states that Joseph offered to divorce her, which was required to end a betrothal in that day. His desire to do so quietly was only for Mary's sake to protect her from public disgrace. Even amid such great personal doubt and question, Joseph put Mary first. He loved her sacrificially and unconditionally, even in his darkest moment.

What quickly became obvious was that God had taken great care to choose a man of incredible character to be the earthly father to His Son. God had been watching and testing Joseph all his life—for this moment. But wait. The story gets better.

As he considered this, an angel of the Lord appeared to him in a dream. "Joseph, son of David," the angel said, "do not be afraid to take Mary as your wife. For the child within her was conceived by the Holy Spirit. And she will have a son, and you are to name him Jesus, for he will save his people from their sins." ... When Joseph woke up, he did as the angel of the Lord commanded and took Mary as his wife. But he did not have sexual relations with her until her son was born. And Joseph named him Jesus. (Matthew 1:20–21, 24–25)

An important point we cannot miss is that the angel didn't say anything in his message that required Joseph to abstain; in fact, he said to "take Mary as your wife." Such a statement would imply all the privileges of marriage. Joseph evidently made a personal choice and sacrifice out of respect for God's plan. He wanted to stay in God's will while staying out of God's way.

With Joseph given the responsibility of raising Jesus, God's making provision for the family would make sense. Remember the gold, frankincense, and myrrh the Magi brought when Christ was a toddler? Yes, those were elaborate gifts that wealthy astronomers brought as worship offerings, but God also provided these as practical assets to finance the family. Those treasures would have provided a nice income for many years. God provided for and honored Joseph's amazing trust and obedience by taking care of his family.

Let's glean a few challenges and inspirations from Joseph's life of dedication to God, Mary, and Jesus:

- Joseph's service and integrity brought one of the greatest assignments any man on earth has ever received.
- Sacrificial love, especially in marriage, always involves a man constantly dying to self. From the moment we met Joseph, we saw how much he loved Mary.
- A man after God's heart works to stay in God's will while staying out of God's way. Joseph's faithful balance was constant.
- Obedience to God is invisible faith put in visible action. Joseph listened to Mary and God, taking action every time.
- God will always provide for what He promises.

When Christmas rolls around, pay a little more attention to the overlooked man in the manger scene. His life of service to our Lord deserves our respect and reverence.

My biggest assignment to serve God in faith came when:

_____

_____

_____

_____

_____

_____

I believe the person or place God is calling me to serve Him today in faith is:

_____

_____

_____

_____

_____

_____

"*Heavenly Father, what an amazing responsibility You gave Joseph to raise Your Son. In following his and Christ's example, help me to sacrificially love, serve, stay in Your will while staying out of Your way, and put my faith into visible action. In Jesus' name, amen.*"

MEMORY VERSE

JOSEPH WAS A MAN WHO ALWAYS DID WHAT WAS RIGHT.

- MATTHEW 1:19 GNT-

**OUR TESTS IN THE PAST
PREPARE US FOR OUR ASSIGNMENTS
IN THE FUTURE.**

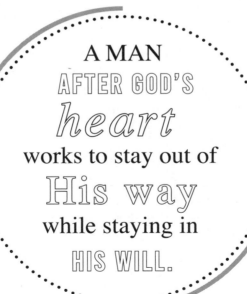

A MAN
AFTER GOD'S
heart
works to stay out of
His way
while staying in
HIS WILL.

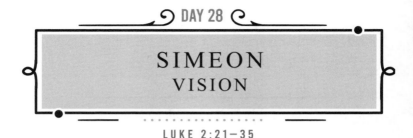

SIMEON
VISION

LUKE 2:21–35

During the time when Jesus was born, forty days after the birth of a male child, the mother had to present herself at the Temple for purification. The couple was to also present a firstborn son for consecration to the service of the Lord. That requirement was the reason for Joseph and Mary coming to the Temple in Luke 2.

Verse 25 introduces Simeon as "righteous and devout." These words typically indicate that a man had a good reputation with God and also with his fellow man. He was known to follow the ways of God while also being upright and honest in the community. This was not about position or title, but rather describing deeply personal qualities.

A fascinating part of Simeon's story is when verse 25 states "the Holy Spirit was upon him." Verse 27 also adds "the Spirit led him to the Temple." Even though we know the Holy Spirit is one-third of the Trinity, He is not officially introduced into the disciples' community until after Christ's ascension, which would have been thirty-three years later. This intentional attachment of the Spirit to Simeon marked his life as unique and special.

Most Jewish people had the expectation that the Messiah would ride in on a white horse, wielding a sword and shining in brilliant heavenly light, to overthrow the government; they believed He would rescue and restore Israel to a permanent state of wealth and power. Imagine the struggle of faith for Simeon as he grew older yet believed in God's promise that he would get to see the Messiah. Now imagine the day that Simeon went to the Temple out of obedience and saw this couple with a newborn. He somehow sensed God tell him, "*That* child is *the* Messiah."

How many couples with babies were in the Temple courtyard that day? How did Simeon know? For him to believe that a helpless baby was actually the Messiah had to be completely God-inspired, yet he had the choice to believe or not. But what an amazing and awe-inspired moment when he walked up to Joseph and Mary, carefully took Jesus in his arms, cradled him to his chest, and worshiped. Simeon's faith became sight.

Simeon held his Savior who would one day hold him and lead him to his home in Heaven.

"Sovereign Lord, now let your servant die in peace, as you have promised. I have seen your salvation, which you have prepared for all people. He is a light to reveal God to the nations, and he is the glory of your people Israel!" Jesus' parents were amazed at what was being said about him. Then Simeon blessed them, and he said to Mary, the baby's mother, "This child is destined to cause many in Israel to fall, and many others to rise. He has

been sent as a sign from God, but many will oppose him. As a result, the deepest thoughts of many hearts will be revealed. And a sword will pierce your very soul." (Luke 2:29–35)

Simeon knew that God had fulfilled His promise. His role on earth was done. Simeon had not only seen the Savior but salvation itself. He held Jesus, so he didn't need this world anymore. Many people in the Gospels had a public encounter with Christ, but Simeon had a very private and personal encounter.

Simeon embraced Christ simply for who He was—just for showing up, for coming to earth. Jesus hadn't done anything yet. He hadn't healed. He hadn't performed a miracle. He hadn't cast out a demon. He hadn't challenged the Pharisees. He hadn't forgiven anyone's sins or died in their place. Simeon worshiped Jesus not because of what Jesus could do for him or what he would receive, but just because He had come.

One thing I believe God will do in my life that I have not yet seen is:

_____

_____

_____

_____

_____

_____

I can better reflect my personal worship of Christ to others by:

_____

_____

_____

_____

_____

_____

"Heavenly Father, thank You for the living example of Jesus, but thank You also for the Holy Spirit who is alive in my life. Please speak to me and help me to fulfill everything You desire my life to accomplish between now and Heaven. In Jesus' name, amen."

MEMORY VERSE

Write your name in the blank to personalize and memorize this adaptation of today's verse:

_____

WAS RIGHTEOUS AND DEVOUT AND ...
THE HOLY SPIRIT WAS UPON HIM.
- LUKE 2:25, ADAPTED -

LEADERS
SEE WHAT OTHERS CAN'T,
EMBRACE WHAT OTHERS WON'T,
AND SPEAK WHAT OTHERS DON'T.

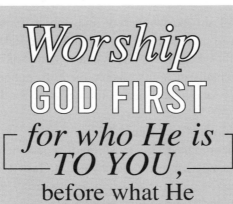

Worship GOD FIRST *for who He is TO YOU,* before what He can do for you.

JOHN THE BAPTIST
RESOLUTE

MATTHEW 3

A man to whom we are introduced early on in all four Gospels is John, a.k.a. John the Baptist. The fact that each writer included him proves his great importance to God's plan. Literally from before his conception to his death, from the prophecy of the angel to Zechariah to the night that Herod was duped into ordering his execution, John was an integral part of Jesus' life.

In Matthew 3, the introduction of John's ministry is quite a scene. Very rough around the edges, John lived in the Judean wilderness and his clothes were woven from coarse camel hair. His diet was wild honey, likely meaning taken directly from beehives, and locusts. (Maybe the honey was a dipping sauce for the locusts?)

John was drawing a curious crowd out at the Jordan River, but then once people heard his message of repentance from sin and about the coming Messiah, many began to profess belief in God and be baptized. Of course, when the Pharisees and Sadducees heard about the competition, they had to come out among the sinners to see what was brewing. When John saw them, he boldly called them out in front of the crowds for their selfish behavior and told them Jesus was on His way.

Then Jesus went from Galilee to the Jordan River to be baptized by John. But John tried to talk him out of it. "I am the one who needs to be baptized by you," he said, "so why are you coming to me?" But Jesus said, "It should be done, for we must carry out all that God requires." So John agreed to baptize him. After his baptism, as Jesus came up out of the water, the heavens were opened and he saw the Spirit of God descending like a dove and settling on him. And a voice from heaven said, "This is my dearly loved Son, who brings me great joy." (Matthew 3:13–17)

John had been preaching boldly *from* faith, *in* faith, *about* faith, believing the Messiah was coming but not knowing *when* He would come. Every day he must have gone out to the river, preached, and baptized, wondering if *that* day would be *the* day. Being faithful to the message he was given, he just kept going. Days came and went. No Jesus.

But then one day, there He was. Like Simeon, he just *knew*. God let John have eyes to see Jesus for who He was, and that the time had come. Imagine being the man given the great privilege of being in the river with Jesus, holding His head and His hands—the head that would one day hold the crown of thorns and the hands that would one day be nailed to the cross—and baptizing Him? Imagine being given the amazing and miraculous experience of seeing the Holy Spirit in the form of a dove descending upon Christ, and then hearing the audible voice of God? What an incredible moment in history and eternity! What a privilege to reward John for his bold faith and lifetime committed to the Gospel.

John's life evidently never had many normal, easy, comfortable moments. He never lived a conventional, ordinary life. He never tasted wealth or worldly success. He never knew the power and fame of man. But few men have ever been given the incredible opportunities that John was provided to see the Kingdom of God literally on earth and on into eternity. The only reason John is not considered the first Christian martyr is because he died for the faith just before Jesus redeemed the world on the cross.

"As John was finishing his ministry he asked, 'Do you think I am the Messiah? No, I am not! But he is coming soon—and I'm not even worthy to be his slave and untie the sandals on his feet.'" (The Apostle Paul in Acts 13:25)

My boldest moment in my faith in Jesus came when:

_____

_____

_____

_____

_____

_____

A situation where I need God to give me His boldness right now is:

_____

_____

_____

_____

_____

_____

"Heavenly Father, I need more of John's unashamed boldness to share the Gospel and call out evil in the world. Empower me through Your Spirit to take every opportunity to allow You to show in my life and share You with my world. In Jesus' name, amen."

MEMORY VERSE

Write your name in the blank to personalize and memorize this adaptation of today's verse:

Know that because of your relationship with Jesus, God can say this about you as well:

_____

IS MY DEARLY LOVED SON, WHO BRINGS ME GREAT JOY."

- MATTHEW 3:17, ADAPTED -

**LEADERS KNOW
WHEN TO HUG A NECK
AND WHEN TO KICK A BUTT.**

Only the

Holy Spirit

CAN GUIDE US

in the balance of
love and truth,
TRUTH AND LOVE.

FOUR FRIENDS
ON A ROOF
INNOVATIVE

LUKE 5:17–26

Jesus had come back to Capernaum and was staying at a certain home there. Word traveled fast that the Healer and Teacher was back in town. People just kept showing up until the house was packed with people and a crowd gathered outside, trying to get in.

When four men who had a paralyzed friend heard that Jesus was back, they decided to get him into His presence as soon as possible. They placed the man on a mat, much like a stretcher, with each grabbing a corner. But when they arrived at the house, they saw a major roadblock: no way to get into the house through the crowd.

These guys refused to be beaten, and their obvious love for their friend was a huge motivation. One of the guys had a crazy idea. He saw a path up to the roof and knew the tiles could be removed to make a temporary portal for them. They all agreed. We don't know the condition of their friend other than his being paralyzed, so you have to imagine if he was able, he might have warned, "I don't know, guys. This seems kind of crazy. Please don't drop me off this roof and make my life worse than it already is!"

Once up on the roof, they began to systematically remove the tiles to create a hole large enough to lower their friend down in front of Jesus. Now if this was a movie, the camera angle would switch to inside the house as daylight began to shine through. Imagine everyone looking up to see these guys peering down into the house. Did the crowd object? Did the owner of the home run out and try to stop them? Were people dusting off debris that was falling down from the roof?

Finally, they had a large enough opening to feel safe about lowering their friend down.

Then they lowered the sick man on his mat down into the crowd, right in front of Jesus. Seeing their faith, Jesus said to the man, "Young man, your sins are forgiven." (Luke 5:19–20)

We have to wonder what Jesus thought about seeing this man on a mat being lowered down in front of Him. What an incredible response that He "saw their faith." These guys were creative, proactive, and innovative. They didn't let a crowded house stop them from getting their beloved friend in front of Jesus. They took Him to the front of the line!

Notice Jesus did not say "You are healed," but rather "Your sins are forgiven." While we are not sure why He responded that way, we quickly see that the teachers of religious law took immediate issue with His words, as they most often did.

189

And what must the four friends have been wondering? "We've gone to all this trouble just to get in the middle of a religious squabble? Hey, Jesus, uh, what about our buddy here?" Then the leaders proudly and arrogantly cried, "Blasphemy!"

Jesus knew what they were thinking, so he asked them, "Why do you question this in your hearts? Is it easier to say 'Your sins are forgiven,' or 'Stand up and walk'? So I will prove to you that the Son of Man has the authority on earth to forgive sins." Then Jesus turned to the paralyzed man and said, "Stand up, pick up your mat, and go home!" And immediately, as everyone watched, the man jumped up, picked up his mat, and went home praising God. Everyone was gripped with great wonder and awe, and they praised God, exclaiming, "We have seen amazing things today!" (Luke 5:22–26)

The mood of the crowd immediately changed when they witnessed the miracle. The four friends got exactly what they had wanted for their friend and experienced what they had worked so hard to experience. And yet again, Jesus closed the mouths of the Pharisees. But the big winner was the paralyzed man who walked out healed physically and spiritually.

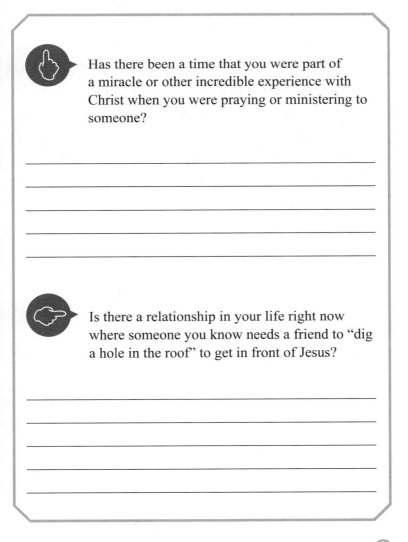

Has there been a time that you were part of a miracle or other incredible experience with Christ when you were praying or ministering to someone?

_____

_____

_____

_____

_____

Is there a relationship in your life right now where someone you know needs a friend to "dig a hole in the roof" to get in front of Jesus?

_____

_____

_____

_____

_____

"Heavenly Father, thank You for my friends who I know would help me like the man's four friends. Please help me to express my faith to help others and be that kind of creative, proactive, and innovative friend. In Jesus' name, amen."

MEMORY VERSE

A REAL FRIEND STICKS CLOSER THAN A BROTHER.

- PROVERBS 18:24 -

**LEADERS CONSTANTLY FIND NEW WAYS TO BE
CREATIVE, PROACTIVE, AND INNOVATIVE.**

Walking daily
WITH GOD
will lead to wonder,
awe, praise, and saying,
"We have seen
amazing
THINGS TODAY!"

CENTURION
CONVICTION

MATTHEW 8:5–13

The strongest opposition to Jesus and biggest roadblock in His ministry and message to the people was the religious leaders of the day. Time and time again throughout the Gospels we see them trying to trick Him into a theological trap or questioning His authority. The vast majority of times Jesus expressed righteous anger and frustration was toward the Pharisees and Sadducees, because of how they spiritually oppressed the people and misrepresented His Father.

Because of this constant battle, Jesus often expressed great joy when one of the people showed faith and understanding in Him and His message. One day as He walked into Capernaum, a centurion—a Roman officer, a Gentile, a hated enemy of the people—walked up to Jesus in the street. Humbly, he asked if the Lord would heal his servant who was suffering from some unknown illness. Seemingly without hesitation, Jesus offered to go to the officer's home. The response of the centurion was surprising.

But the officer said, "Lord, I am not worthy to have you come into my home. Just say the word from where you are, and my servant will be healed. I know this because I am under the authority of my superior officers, and I have authority over my soldiers. I only need to say, 'Go,' and they go, or 'Come,' and they come. And if I say to my slaves, 'Do this,' they do it." (Matthew 8:8–9)

Keep in mind that Jesus had been teaching in parables to allow people the opportunity to understand God's Kingdom and why He had come. He had become accustomed to misunderstanding or misinterpretation of His motives and message. The officer understood and operated under a strict chain of command and authority. He had confidence that if he told a soldier to go and do a task, that order would be carried out because of who the officer was and the power he held. This man simply applied that working knowledge to Jesus in the spiritual realm. Such a level of connecting the dots and acceptance was inspiring for that day and still is today.

When Jesus heard this, he was amazed. Turning to those who were following him, he said, "I tell you the truth, I haven't seen faith like this in all Israel! And I tell you this, that many Gentiles will come from all over the world—from east and west—and sit down with Abraham, Isaac, and Jacob at the feast in the Kingdom of Heaven. But many Israelites—those for whom the Kingdom was prepared—will be thrown into outer darkness, where there will be weeping and gnashing of teeth." (Matthew 8:10–12)

Imagine for a moment how shocked everyone must have been to hear Jesus award the top prize for spiritual faith in all Israel to a Roman army officer! No one would have seen that coming.

But the stark reality was the statement was 100 percent true. This man accepted and believed Jesus' heavenly authority as well as His ability to miraculously heal.

But then Jesus' realization gave the inspiration and opportunity to make an extremely powerful prophetic point: Gentiles were not only going to come to faith, but one day they would be seated with the greatest Jewish forefathers. Then He went on to the other side of the coin: Many of the very people God wanted to inherit His Kingdom would not be seated at that table, but be thrown into Hell because they would not believe who He was.

Such a declaration would have been a total game changer. This kind of bold proclamation was also what caused Jesus to be increasingly hated by the religious leaders. Here in the earliest place in the New Testament, Jesus actually revealed the heart of the Gospel that we later hear from Paul: "Everyone who calls on the name of the Lord will be saved" (Romans 10:13). His message was not about *who* you are, but *what* you believe about Him.

Jesus then turned His attention back to the officer and completed the work of the *second* miracle, the *first* being the man's expression of faith. We must not miss that Jesus did *exactly* as the man requested—right then, right there, in a moment.

Then Jesus said to the Roman officer, "Go back home. Because you believed, it has happened." And the young servant was healed that same hour. (Matthew 8:13)

The biggest step toward and expression of faith in Jesus I have ever taken in my life was:

_____

_____

_____

_____

_____

_____

One circumstance today where I want to hear Jesus say, "Because you have believed, it has happened," is:

_____

_____

_____

_____

_____

_____

"Heavenly Father, help my faith to grow to the point where I can confidently express to You, "Just say the word from where You are" about anything I pray. I want to have the kind of faith that surprises and pleases You in our crazy culture. But no matter what Your answer, give me the strength and boldness to always trust You. In Jesus' name, amen."

MEMORY VERSE

"Because you believed, it has happened."

- Matthew 8:13 -

CONFIDENT, STRONG LEADERS
UNDERSTAND, ACCEPT, AND OPERATE
IN AUTHORITY,
WITH THOSE ABOVE
AND THOSE BELOW.

BELIEFS
will always
DETERMINE
who we
BECOME.

PRODIGAL SON
SUBMISSIVE

LUKE 15:11–32

In the day when Jesus taught this timeless parable found in Luke 15, the family estate and business would go to the sons when the father died or was unable to oversee it any longer. One of this man's two sons came to him and requested his inheritance, which would have been hurtful. The inference was "I don't want to wait around until you die, Dad. I want what's coming to me right now. And I'm not sticking around to help the family business. I'm out of here."

Even so, the father in Jesus' story complied with the son's request. We don't know whether he had to sell some livestock or land to get the son's portion, but the son left home to seek the high life with "all his money," as verse 13 states. Like an ignorant, immature lottery winner, he quickly lived large and fell hard. Whether lavish spending, foolish gambling, or getting swindled by bad men and loose women, the young man ended up broke and far from home. To make matters worse, famine struck the land.

Likely because the only job skill he ever had was farming, he found work feeding a man's pigs. With everyone else trying to survive, the young man had no food and no one to give him a handout. Finally, he had a moment of clarity when he began to look at the pigs' food as his only source. With his stomach empty and his pride gone, he had the lucid thought to go home and ask his father to hire him as a servant. He had given up his legal and ethical right to sonship, so working as a field hand was a long shot, but at least a shot. Using his last option, he headed for his father's home.

"And while he was still a long way off, his father saw him coming. Filled with love and compassion, he ran to his son, embraced him, and kissed him. His son said to him, 'Father, I have sinned against both heaven and you, and I am no longer worthy of being called your son.'" (Luke 15:20–21)

We must not miss the many nuances here of what Jesus communicated about our Father in Heaven. For this dad to see his son coming from "a long way off," he had to be hoping, believing, and watching for his return. The father's response was not to stand with his arms crossed, glaring, until his wayward son walked up so he could say, "So you're back! I expected this from you." Far too many men carry this "angry dad" image of God. This is one of the major reasons Jesus gave us this parable: to refute and correct that common paradigm.

The son's response was just as crucial to the reconciliation. The young man did not waste a single word, offering, "I have sinned and hurt you and God"—a full repentant confession. Then the reality: "I gave up my sonship so my only option to come back onto the family estate is as a hired servant."

"But his father said to the servants, 'Quick! Bring the finest robe in the house and put it on him. Get a ring for his finger and sandals for his feet. And kill the calf we have been fattening. We must celebrate with a feast, for this son of mine was dead and has now returned to life. He was lost, but now he is found.' So the party began." (Luke 15:22–24)

The father ignored the son's request and brought him back to full sonship. The robe and the ring were signs of fully restored authority and acceptance.

When we confess our sin, do you think our Father wants us to wallow in guilt and shame? Do you think while everyone was eating and dancing at the celebration, that the prodigal's father wanted his son to be moping in the corner, continuing to punish himself for his failure? No, the father wanted his son to receive everything he had offered to be restored and celebrate at his own party. When we ask God for forgiveness, we must do the same. We cannot react the way we *feel* we should, but the way God would have us through what *He has provided* in Jesus.

Jesus' parable was the last of three offered to shed light on God's love as Father and His response to gathering His lost children. This passage has so many rich truths to help us grasp God's grace and learn to receive His forgiveness and love.

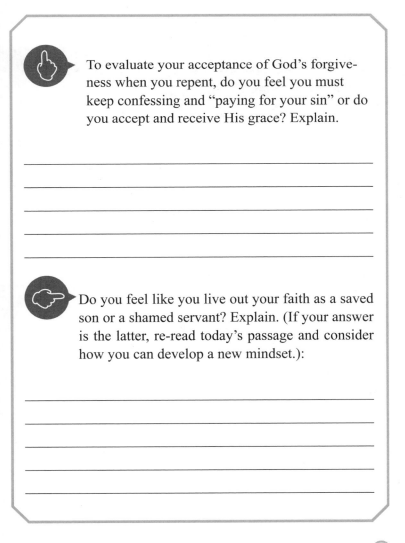

To evaluate your acceptance of God's forgiveness when you repent, do you feel you must
keep confessing and "paying for your sin" or do
you accept and receive His grace? Explain.

_____

_____

_____

_____

_____

Do you feel like you live out your faith as a saved
son or a shamed servant? Explain. (If your answer
is the latter, re-read today's passage and consider
how you can develop a new mindset.):

_____

_____

_____

_____

_____

"Heavenly Father, thank You for this amazing parable to give me a correct concept of Your love and grace, forgiveness and acceptance. Teach me more and more how to love as Your son with full authority, as You have freely given me. In Jesus' name, amen."

MEMORY VERSE

Write your name in the blank to personalize and memorize this adaptation of today's verse:

"FOR _____

WAS DEAD AND HAS COME BACK TO LIFE! HE WAS LOST, BUT NOW HE IS FOUND!"

- LUKE 15:32 -

**LEADERS ARE
BRIDGE BUILDERS,
NOT BRIDGE BURNERS.**

God invites us to be

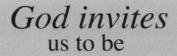

HIS SONS

who serve Him

OUT OF LOVE,
not slaves who serve
Him out of fear.

CRIMINAL ON THE CROSS

REDEMPTION

LUKE 23:32–43

In today's title, like the centurion, we aren't given his name. If you are familiar with this story, you might also ask how this man could be included on a list of biblical leaders. Valid question. In many ways, this exchange in Scripture says more about Jesus than the man. However, there was another criminal hanging on the other side of Christ who showed us the difference in men. He expressed the same hatred for and lack of belief in Christ that the soldiers and the crowd had on that fateful Friday. So the criminal's choice is his leadership quality, the one that brought about Jesus' promise of salvation—the first recorded salvation that actually began at the cross.

This amazing encounter in Scripture became possibly the best real-life example of what God will receive as a prayer for salvation. Bloody and badly beaten from the cat-of-nine-tails whip, Christ was hanging on the cross between two criminals, although we are not told their actual charges. At the point they were introduced, what they did no longer mattered because they were being executed. Jesus was innocent of all wrongdoing, while the two men on each side were found guilty.

Read the fascinating exchange between Christ and the two men as they were all suffering horrific, painful, very slow deaths.

One of the criminals hanging beside him scoffed, "So you're the Messiah, are you? Prove it by saving yourself—and us, too, while you're at it!" But the other criminal protested, "Don't you fear God even when you have been sentenced to die? We deserve to die for our crimes, but this man hasn't done anything wrong." Then he said, "Jesus, remember me when you come into your Kingdom." And Jesus replied, "I assure you, today you will be with me in paradise." (Luke 23:39–43)

These five verses offer us the two opposing responses that mankind can and will ever make throughout history regarding Jesus.

- Against or accept
- Insult or invite
- Reject or receive

But Christ, hanging in between the two extremes, died for *both* sides. Because we are all hopeless sinners, He made the choice available to *all*.

The first man was full of anger and bitterness. His words were threatening and filled with mocking disbelief. This same voice screams throughout our culture today, as loud as ever. How dare someone claim to be a Savior! That mindset was alive then and today.

The second man was immediately remorseful and repentant. The most amazing thing that he said was the first thing out of his mouth—his defense of Jesus and His innocence. But this criminal's last words are some of the most humbling and intriguing in all of Scripture. He called Jesus by name, expressing great faith by stating He knew Christ had a kingdom and would be returning to Heaven. Then he didn't actually ask for salvation, likely because he felt his sin was too great to be saved. He simply requested that Jesus remember him. His words were more like, "Please don't forget about me." He didn't say "Save me," but "Remember me."

Jesus took the request to another level and said, "Not only will I remember you, but on this very day you will be with Me." Imagine for a moment suffering a terrifying and painful death, gasping to take another breath, fighting to stay alive, and hearing the Son of God tell you that when you can no longer lift your chest up to take another breath, you will be in paradise. The lost could be forever found in a simple, single sentence.

We cannot miss the fact that Jesus never responded to the first thief's scornful insults. He only spoke to the one who expressed faith. Even while suffering and dying on the cross, Jesus allowed the freedom to choose Him or not. The bottom line is without surrender, salvation will not occur. We see clearly in this scene that the intent of the heart is far more crucial than the choice of words. The right phrase does not save—Jesus does. There is no magic formula, but there is a merciful Father.

Is there any part of the second criminal's response to Jesus that reminds you of your own salvation?

_____

_____

_____

_____

_____

_____

How can you keep your humility and gratitude alive and fresh in your heart for the fact that Jesus "remembered you"?

_____

_____

_____

_____

_____

_____

"Heavenly Father, I was just as guilty in my shame and sin as those criminals. Thank You for allowing me to see my need for You to become like the second criminal and no longer live in the state of the first criminal. Embolden me to share how You have saved me and that Your heart is for all to accept and receive Your gift of salvation. In Jesus' name, amen."

MEMORY VERSE

FOR GOD SAYS,
"AT JUST THE RIGHT TIME, I HEARD YOU.
ON THE DAY OF SALVATION, I HELPED YOU."

- 2 CORINTHIANS 6:2 -

**A LEADER SPEAKS UP,
DEFENDS THE INNOCENT,
AND RECOGNIZES HIS OWN WRONGS.**

The cross
of
CHRIST
is the only and ultimate
DIVIDING LINE
IN THE
HUMAN
race.

TWO MEN
FROM EMMAUS
WITNESS

LUKE 24:13–34

On the day the disciples discovered that Jesus was no longer in the grave, two men who had followed Him decided to leave Jerusalem. Discouraged and not understanding the events that had taken place, they decided there was nothing left for them there and headed back home to Emmaus.

Walking down the dusty road, seemingly out of nowhere another man came up to them. As He approached, He asked, "What are you discussing so intently as you walk along?" One of the men, Cleopas, stopped in his tracks and showed that he was in no mood for small talk. Sarcastically, he answered, "You must be the only person in Jerusalem who hasn't heard about all the things that have happened there the last few days." "What things?" the stranger asked. "The things that happened to Jesus, the man from Nazareth," Cleopas responded.

The two men then proceeded to explain about Jesus' miracles and teaching, and then His trial and crucifixion. They went on to express great disappointment and disillusionment that the man must have only been a prophet; they had hoped He was the Messiah sent to rescue Israel. They concluded by telling how the disciples had gone to the tomb and found His body was missing, and how angels had reported He was alive.

The stranger began to speak, taking the men all the way back to Moses, through the prophets, and connected the dots to how all of Scripture pointed to Christ. When He was done and they had arrived in Emmaus, the two men asked the stranger to come to their home, which was the custom of the day for neighborly hospitality. Then, as they sat down to dinner, a mystical and miraculous moment occurred.

The man to whom they had been talking for hours, now took some bread, broke it, blessed it, and handed it to them. In that moment, the men realized the stranger was Jesus!

Suddenly, their eyes were opened, and they recognized him. And at that moment he disappeared! They said to each other, "Didn't our hearts burn within us as he talked with us on the road and explained the Scriptures to us?" And within the hour they were on their way back to Jerusalem. There they found the eleven disciples and the others who had gathered with them. (Luke 24:31–33)

How amazing that Jesus would pursue these men and teach them! Even though they had missed the message of the cross, they became confirmed eyewitnesses of His resurrection. Can you imagine walking with Jesus for miles and having Him explain how all of Scripture fits together to confirm Him?

213

When the two men reached the other disciples in Jerusalem, they were able to add to the excitement of firsthand experience. And just when the story couldn't get any better, right in the middle of their testimony, Jesus appeared in the room with them all (verse 36).

Something deep in every person's soul cries out for an explanation of how they fit into this grand plan called life. Just as Jesus walked up and engaged the two men in conversation, then after hearing their concerns explained Himself to them, we too can tell others about His life in us.

Today, we'll merge the Upward and Outward questions by offering you a very simple way to write out your testimony. Complete these open-ended sentences so you can share your story.

My life before Christ was:

_____

_____

_____

_____

I came to know Jesus through/because of:

_____

_____

_____

_____

_____

My relationship with Jesus has changed my life by:

_____

_____

_____

_____

_____

Today, God is working in my life by/through:

_____

_____

_____

_____

_____

"Dear Jesus, thank You for coming after me, finding me on my road, and making sure I knew You. Help me to be a part of someone else's story by sharing mine whenever I have the opportunity. In Your name, amen."

MEMORY VERSE

Write your name in the blank to personalize and memorize this adaptation of today's verse:

_____

IS CHRIST'S AMBASSADOR;
AS THOUGH GOD WAS MAKING HIS APPEAL THROUGH ME.
- 2 CORINTHIANS 5:20 NIV, ADAPTED -

LEADERS DISPLAY
A PASSIONATE HEART,
A PATIENT SPIRIT,
AND A PURPOSEFUL MIND.

God
PURSUES
–HIS–
children
with
PASSION, PATIENCE,
AND PURPOSE.

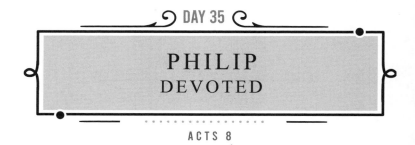

PHILIP
DEVOTED

ACTS 8

As persecution against Jesus' disciples heightened and after Saul martyred Stephen, the believers scattered from Jerusalem into Judea and Samaria. But the persecution actually backfired and the Gospel spread, because everywhere they went, the believers ministered and shared the message about Jesus.

Philip had gone into Samaria, and people there had responded to the Gospel. When Peter and John decided to return to Jerusalem, the Spirit gave Philip specific instructions and directions. Like so often in Scripture, God said which way to go but did not share why to go. The directions were to "go south down the desert road that runs from Jerusalem to Gaza" (Acts 8:26).

Philip soon came upon an interesting sight—an obvious dignitary traveling down the road in a carriage. The treasurer of Ethiopia who served the queen was returning from Jerusalem. Philip sensed the Spirit tell him to go walk beside the carriage. He then heard an interesting sound—the treasurer reading the words of Isaiah from a scroll, which "just so happened" to be chapter 53:7–8, which prophesies about Jesus.

Sensitive to the Spirit, rather than running up to start preaching or handing out answers, Philip simply asked the man, "Do you understand what you are reading?" By asking such a question, if the man had been prideful or private, he could have responded with a simple yes or even ignored him. But the Spirit knew what Philip didn't yet know.

The man replied, "How can I, unless someone instructs me?" And he urged Philip to come up into the carriage and sit with him. ... The eunuch asked Philip, "Tell me, was the prophet talking about himself or someone else?" So beginning with this same Scripture, Philip told him the Good News about Jesus. (Acts 8:31, 34–35)

As the two came upon a body of water, the treasurer asked Philip to baptize him, just as Jesus had been baptized. Next is one of those brief miraculous moments we can easily miss in the Bible, but we need to pay attention to how serious God has always been about getting the Gospel out to everyone throughout the world.

When they came up out of the water, the Spirit of the Lord snatched Philip away. The eunuch never saw him again but went on his way rejoicing. Meanwhile, Philip found himself farther north at the town of Azotus. He preached the Good News there and in every town along the way until he came to Caesarea. (Acts 8:39–40)

The same Holy Spirit is alive and well today, speaking to Christ's followers in this same manner. And God is just as serious today about getting His Gospel out to the world as He was in that day. Here are four "L" points we can glean from this story of Philip and the Ethiopian treasurer:

1. Listen
   The Holy Spirit knows when and where someone is ready to hear. He can and will show us who to tell about Jesus.

2. Learn
   Like Philip, we must first hear a person's questions and needs. The old saying "People don't care how much you know until they know how much you care" is a crucial precursor to the Gospel.

3. Look—for the gateway to present Jesus
   After Philip asked his question, the man's answer contained his questions. That led Philip to know exactly what to share.

4. Lead—the conversation to Christ
   We are stewards of the Gospel from salvation to Heaven, responsible for the times when He speaks to us to share our faith.

While there is only one Gospel, one Lord, one faith, and one baptism, there can be many inroads and gateways to reach people that are as diverse as we are. God will never ask us to compromise His message but He finds many ways to customize His message to reach people.

The first time I knew that the Lord had brought someone into my life for me to share the Gospel was:

_____

_____

_____

_____

_____

_____

Someone I believe the Lord has brought into my life today that He wants me to share Him with is:

_____

_____

_____

_____

_____

_____

"Heavenly Father, thank You so much for bringing someone into my life to witness to me and share Your message. Thank You that You cared enough about me to make sure someone told me about You. Please give me the sensitivity to Your Spirit to see, hear, and know when You are calling me to share You with others. In Jesus' name, amen."

MEMORY VERSE

*BE READY AT ALL TIMES
TO ANSWER ANYONE
WHO ASKS YOU TO EXPLAIN
THE HOPE YOU HAVE.*

- 1 PETER 3:15 GNT -

LEADERS LISTEN, LEARN, AND LOOK BEFORE THEY LEAP.

66 **I tell** you, open your eyes & **LOOK AT THE FIELDS!** *They are ripe for* **harvest.** 99

JESUS IN JOHN 4:35 NIV

DAY 36

PETER
TRAILBLAZER

ACTS 10 — 11:18

When many people think of the disciple, apostle, and church founder Peter, the scenes around Jesus' crucifixion quickly come to mind. He couldn't stay awake and pray in the Garden of Gethsemane. He was the disciple believed to have cut off the soldier's ear with a sword. And he fulfilled Christ's fateful words when he denied the Lord three times in the courtyard before the rooster crowed.

But through the Holy Spirit's powerful transformation coupled with his obedience, Peter went from the guy who wouldn't speak up for Jesus the night of the trials to God's mouthpiece who wouldn't be silenced. He led thousands to salvation in his public preaching. When you trace Peter's life from the denial of Christ to Pentecost, anyone would have to admit that something major happened to him. He became a man he had never been before. Yet that's exactly what Jesus does when we surrender to Him.

Peter took a massive step of faith, as well as a huge risk, to bring the Gospel to the entire world when no one else had the guts to do so. After Jesus had ascended to Heaven and the disciples were establishing the church, a great division still had to be bridged. The

Jews were God's chosen people, but then there were the Gentiles. Through a vision and miraculous moment, Peter was invited to the home of a Roman centurion named Cornelius. The risk factor was that Jews associating with Gentiles was unlawful. But acting on his word from God, Peter went anyway, entered the soldier's home, and spoke with the entire household.

Then Peter replied, "I see very clearly that God shows no favoritism. In every nation he accepts those who fear him and do what is right. This is the message of Good News for the people of Israel—that there is peace with God through Jesus Christ, who is Lord of all. ... And he ordered us to preach everywhere and to testify that Jesus is the one appointed by God to be the judge of all—the living and the dead. He is the one all the prophets testified about, saying that everyone who believes in him will have their sins forgiven through his name." (Acts 10:34–36, 42–43)

Scripture says the Holy Spirit came upon them all and they were baptized that day. When the news got out and Peter returned to Jerusalem, the other believers there criticized him for crossing the racial and spiritual lines that were firmly in place to keep people divided. So Peter took the new church through the entire story, leaving no details out.

When the others heard this, they stopped objecting and began praising God. They said, "We can see that God has also given the Gentiles the privilege of repenting of their sins and receiving eternal life." (Acts 11:18)

225

This was a major crossroads in history when *everything* changed. Cultural dividing lines were erased because of the Gospel. Jew and Gentile were joining hands for the first time in history. God was telling His leaders that when He meant salvation was for everyone, He truly meant *everyone*! There was no place, no person, and no circumstance He could be kept from saving.

Peter's transformation had brought him from the courtyard, caring only about what people thought of him, unwilling to risk his life, to Cornelius's house, where he cared only about what Jesus wanted him to do, willing to risk his newfound reputation for the sake of the Gospel.

The biggest risk God has ever called me to take was:

_____

_____

_____

_____

_____

I believe the circumstance where God is calling me to risk for Him today is:

_____

_____

_____

_____

_____

_____

"Heavenly Father, thank You that You are the same God who empowered Peter's marvelous transformation. You have done and desire to do the same in and through me. Strengthen me to put You first, obey You, and risk for the sake of Your Kingdom, as Peter did. In Jesus' name, amen."

MEMORY VERSE

"I SEE VERY CLEARLY THAT GOD SHOWS NO FAVORITISM."

- ACTS 10:34 -

LEADERS ARE PIONEERS WHO BLAZE NEW TRAILS
AND TAKE NEW GROUND WHERE OTHERS CAN LIVE.

WITH THE GOSPEL as our foundation WE INVITE everyone INTO THE HOUSE.

PAUL
TRANSFORMATION

ACTS 9:1–31

While the Bible records many divine transformations, Saul-turned-Paul is one of the most dramatic and radical. Saul had overseen Stephen's stoning. Now, as Acts 9 begins, the disciples were spreading the Gospel post-resurrection with Saul publicly seeking their arrest and privately eager to execute them. He saw Jesus' revolution as a threat to the Pharisee's domination of religious life in Jerusalem.

When he received permission for he and his entourage to go to Damascus to hunt down disciples, he had no idea that life as he knew it was about to change forever. On the road, a sudden blinding bright light, not of this world, struck Saul. He immediately fell to the ground.

The glorious light was so bright that he could not see, and he heard a voice ask, "Saul, why are you persecuting Me?" Humbled and frightened, Saul asked, "Who are you, lord?"

And the voice replied, "I am Jesus, the one you are persecuting! Now get up and go into the city, and you will be told what you must do." (Acts 9:5–6)

We must not miss the fact that Jesus did not ask, "Saul, why are you persecuting the church?" He said "persecuting Me." Christ appeared to Saul in person and made his assault very personal, as if to communicate, "You aren't hunting down and killing some organization. These people are My friends and followers."

But the most fascinating aspect of this encounter was that Jesus did not demand that he stop, or even execute Saul. Rather, He gave him a command to go into the city and wait for further instructions. When Jesus and the heavenly light left, blinded Saul's companions led him into Damascus, where he was taken to a certain house to wait. Imagine the shock and fear Saul would have had. Number one, he was blind with no idea if he would ever see again. And two, he was trying to process the experience that the crucified and resurrected Christ had appeared before him and given him explicit instructions. He would now by faith leave the ranks of the Pharisees and join the despised disciples. He would leave behind the life of a religious zealot who hated Christ and take on the love of a radical relationship with Him.

A Christ-follower in Damascus named Ananias was visited by Jesus concerning Saul. When the Lord told him to go to Saul and lay his hand on him and pray to bring back his sight, Ananias knew immediately about the persecutor and his reputation. Yet another very human moment in Scripture. A disciple is told to go find an evil man assigned by the religious leaders to capture and imprison believers. That must have felt like being asked to walk right into a trap.

But the Lord said, "Go, for Saul is my chosen instrument to take my message to the Gentiles and to kings, as well as to the people of Israel." (Acts 9:15)

Jesus did not say, "No, Ananias, it's okay. Don't worry. He won't hurt you." He simply said "Go" and then for the first time, revealed Saul-turned-Paul's new calling.

Ananias obeyed and found Saul. He laid his hands on him and, amazingly, out of love, forgiveness, and grace, called him "brother," fully trusting what Jesus had revealed. Immediately Saul regained his sight. He was baptized and ate. In a very real way, like all of us in the event of salvation, Saul died on that road and Paul was the new man born on the other side. Gathered now with the believers in Damascus, Paul started to preach the Gospel, telling his miraculous story. But Paul's new life also turned the tables on his old life.

All who heard him were amazed. "Isn't this the same man who caused such devastation among Jesus' followers in Jerusalem?" they asked. ... Saul's preaching became more and more powerful, and the Jews in Damascus couldn't refute his proofs that Jesus was indeed the Messiah. (Acts 9:21–22)

All of us as men have things in our past or present that cause us to feel inadequate or ineffective as ministers of the Gospel. If Paul could overcome his past, accept God's forgiveness, and press full force into his calling, we certainly can too.

The most radical sign of transformation in my life because of Christ was:

_____

_____

_____

_____

_____

_____

The one thing from my past that sometimes holds me back and hinders me from freely ministering is:

_____

_____

_____

_____

_____

_____

"Heavenly Father, what You did with Paul is a constant source of inspiration. Thank You that You have transformed my life too. Help me to take my calling for You as seriously as Paul did to reach people in my culture for You. In Jesus' name, amen."

MEMORY VERSE

Write your name in the blank to personalize and
memorize this adaptation of today's verse:

For _____

IS NOT ASHAMED OF THE GOSPEL,
BECAUSE IT IS THE POWER OF GOD
THAT BRINGS SALVATION TO EVERYONE WHO BELIEVES.

- ROMANS 1:16, ADAPTED -

A LEADER ENCOURAGES,
ALLOWS FOR, AND ACCEPTS
THAT ANYONE CAN CHANGE.

Every person's story
THAT ENDS WITH
JESUS
becomes
His-story!

JESUS
MINISTRY

REVELATION 5

The Gospels are our records of Jesus' life and ministry, pre- and post-resurrection. But the book of Revelation contains important messages from Him and facts about Him. One of the most poignant and passionate passages is found in chapter 5. The heavenly setting and imagery are so powerful and worshipful. John's vision allows us to see what takes place in Heaven when the One who left as the Lion of Judah returned home as the Lamb of God.

Today, we will focus fully on Scripture by reading the entire chapter of Revelation 5, along with some correlating Scripture.

Then I saw a scroll in the right hand of the one who was sitting on the throne. There was writing on the inside and the outside of the scroll, and it was sealed with seven seals. And I saw a strong angel, who shouted with a loud voice: "Who is worthy to break the seals on this scroll and open it?" But no one in heaven or on earth or under the earth was able to open the scroll and read it. (vv. 1–3)

Romans 3:10–12: *"No one is righteous—not even one. No one is truly wise; no one is seeking God. All have turned away; all have*

become useless. No one does good, not a single one."

Then I began to weep bitterly because no one was found worthy to open the scroll and read it. But one of the twenty-four elders said to me, "Stop weeping! Look, the Lion of the tribe of Judah, the heir to David's throne, has won the victory. He is worthy to open the scroll and its seven seals." (vv. 4–5)

Isaiah 9:7: *He will rule with fairness and justice from the throne of his ancestor David for all eternity. The passionate commitment of the Lord of Heaven's Armies will make this happen!*

Then I saw a Lamb that looked as if it had been slaughtered, but it was now standing between the throne and the four living beings and among the twenty-four elders. (v.6)

John 1:29: *John saw Jesus coming toward him and said, "Look! The Lamb of God who takes away the sin of the world!"*

He stepped forward and took the scroll from the right hand of the one sitting on the throne. And when he took the scroll, the four living beings and the twenty-four elders fell down before the Lamb. Each one had a harp, and they held gold bowls filled with incense, which are the prayers of God's people. And they sang a new song with these words: "You are worthy to take the scroll and break its seals and open it. For you were slaughtered, and your blood has ransomed people for God from every tribe and language and people and nation. And you have caused them to become a Kingdom of priests for our God. And they will reign on the earth." (vv. 7–10)

Mark 14:24: *And he said to them, "This is my blood, which confirms the covenant between God and his people. It is poured out as a sacrifice for many."*

Then I looked again, and I heard the voices of thousands and millions of angels around the throne and of the living beings and the elders. And they sang in a mighty chorus: "Worthy is the Lamb who was slaughtered—to receive power and riches and wisdom and strength and honor and glory and blessing." And then I heard every creature in heaven and on earth and under the earth and in the sea. They sang: "Blessing and honor and glory and power belong to the one sitting on the throne and to the Lamb forever and ever." And the four living beings said, "Amen!" And the twenty-four elders fell down and worshiped the Lamb. (vv. 11–14)

Isaiah 53:4–5: *Yet it was our weaknesses he carried; it was our sorrows that weighed him down. And we thought his troubles were a punishment from God, a punishment for his own sins! But he was pierced for our rebellion, crushed for our sins. He was beaten so we could be whole. He was whipped so we could be healed.*

The first time I realized all that Jesus had done for me, I felt:

_____

_____

_____

The most powerful aspect of the Gospel that I love to share with people is:

_____

_____

_____

Today, take a few minutes to write out a prayer like a thank-you note to Jesus for His gift of salvation to you.

_____

_____

_____

MEMORY VERSE

Write your name in the blank to personalize and
memorize this adaptation of today's verse:

BUT HE WAS PIERCED FOR

_____ *'S*

REBELLION,

CRUSHED FOR

_____ *'S*

SINS.

HE WAS BEATEN SO

_____

COULD BE WHOLE.

HE WAS WHIPPED SO

_____

COULD BE HEALED.

- ISAIAH 53:5, ADAPTED -

A LEADER LEARNS
WHEN TO SUBMIT,
WHEN TO SACRIFICE,
AND WHEN TO TAKE A STAND.

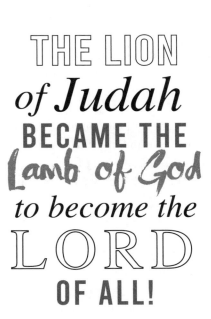

THE LION
of Judah
BECAME THE
Lamb of God
to become the
LORD
OF ALL!

THE FIRST ADAM
PERSONAL CHOICE

GENESIS 2—3

Our final two days are connected, designed to explain the choice we all make every single day of our lives. We start by going back to the beginning in Genesis.

If we claim to follow Christ, then each day that we wake up and God allows us to have life and breath, we must make a decision. Whether conscious of that choice or not, we walk one way or the other. But first, we have to understand how we arrived at this place.

The greatest, most epic battlegrounds in history happened in a garden. In two key places in Scripture, a garden became a battle-field with Heaven and Hell clashing for the soul of man. The first garden, the site of the first battle, was called Eden.

Then the Lord God planted a garden in Eden in the east, and there he placed the man he had made. The Lord God made all sorts of trees grow up from the ground—trees that were beautiful and that produced delicious fruit. In the middle of the garden he placed the tree of life and the tree of the knowledge of good and evil. The Lord God placed the man in the Garden of Eden to tend and watch over it. But the Lord God warned him, "You may freely eat the fruit of every tree in the garden—except the tree of the knowledge of good and evil. If you eat its fruit, you are sure to die." Then the Lord God said, "It is not good for the man to be alone. I will make a helper who is just right for him." (Genesis 2:8–9, 15–18)

When God gave Adam his only law of the Garden, Eve had not even been created yet. God also allowed his archenemy onto the same earth where his most prized creation lived in communion with Him. In His sovereignty and omniscience, He knew a battle was inevitably going to take place in His garden—His son against His enemy.

While God's command regarding the tree of the knowledge of good and evil applied to Eve too, God apparently left the authority and responsibility up to Adam to:

- Provide the truth to her
- Protect her
- Prioritize her

What God was doing for Adam, He wanted Adam to do for Eve. But as with all humanity, God gave Adam the choice, by free will, of whether to obey or not.

The serpent was the shrewdest of all the wild animals the Lord God had made. One day he asked the woman, "Did God really say you must not eat the fruit from any of the trees in the garden?" "Of course we may eat fruit from the trees in the garden," the woman replied. "It's only the fruit from the tree in the middle of the garden that we are not allowed to eat. God said, 'You must not eat it or even touch it; if you do, you will die.'" "You won't die!" the serpent replied to the woman. "God knows that your eyes will be opened as soon as you eat it, and you will be like God, knowing both good and evil." The woman was convinced. She saw that the tree was beautiful and its fruit looked delicious, and she wanted the wisdom it would give her. So she took some of the fruit and ate it. Then she gave some to her husband, who was with her, and he ate it, too. (Genesis 3:1–6)

Consider for a moment how things might be different if, when the Enemy confronted Eve and Adam heard him trying to manipulate His bride, Adam would have stepped in between her and the serpent. He then took the authority that God had given him over everything in the garden, rebuked the Enemy, shut him down, and walked away with Eve. Unharmed. Innocent. Sinless.

Applying all we know of God in Scripture and what He told Adam before Eve was created, we can safely say that God intended for Adam to:

- Protect his bride
- Purge the Enemy
- Pursue God's glory

But he didn't. In his first battle with the Enemy, Adam lost, not because he didn't fight hard enough, but simply because he didn't lift a finger. In fact, the only choice Adam made was to eat.

Like Adam, we make sinful choices daily to continue the:

- Compliance with the same Enemy (choosing sin over God)
- Complacency in the same manner (being lazy and apathetic, not proactive)
- Cowardice of the First Adam (retreating rather than advancing, procrastinating rather than protecting)

Choosing to eat forbidden fruit rather than fight to honor God is the way of the First Adam, the source of our sin nature.

Why do you suppose the widespread narrative from the Garden in both the religious and secular worlds became Eve getting all the blame for sin?

_____

_____

_____

_____

_____

_____

_____

Write down some ways you can practically apply the three Ps and the three Cs to challenge your own life:

_____

_____

_____

_____

_____

_____

_____

"Heavenly Father, thank You that You didn't leave us when we ran away, but came after us. Even though that was, of course, not me, I know I still make that choice every time when I sin, yet You still come after me. Thank You for pursuing me, no matter what choice I make. In Jesus' name, amen."

MEMORY VERSE

WHEN ADAM SINNED, SIN ENTERED THE WORLD.

- ROMANS 5:12 -

**LEADERSHIP REQUIRES KEEPING
THE BIG PICTURE IN FOCUS
EVEN WHEN THE LENS GETS DIRTY.**

WHEN GOD
grants
authority
TO ACT,
He gives
access to
HIS ATTRIBUTES
and answers.

THE LAST ADAM
PERSONAL CHANGE

MARK 14:32–42, 1 CORINTHIANS 15:45–49

Today is a continuation and finale of the First Adam message from Scripture. Yesterday we talked about how we got here. Now let's discuss how we get to where we are going and truly discover real change.

With the first garden being Eden, the second garden, the site of the second and final battle, was called Gethsemane. In this story, as in the Garden of Eden, we have the same elements and dynamics:

- Garden
- Man (Jesus—all God yet all man, with a choice)
- Enemy
- Battle
- God-given authority
- Opportunity to glorify or deny God

Gethsemane is Eden revisited. And Eden redeemed.

They went to the olive grove called Gethsemane, and Jesus said, "Sit here while I go and pray." He took Peter, James, and John with him, and he became deeply troubled and distressed. He told them, "My soul is crushed with grief to the point of death. Stay here and keep watch with me." He went on a little farther and fell to the ground. He prayed that, if it were possible, the awful hour awaiting him might pass him by. "Abba, Father," he cried out, "everything is possible for you. Please take this cup of suffering away from me." (Mark 14:32–36)

While we see no record here of the physical presence of the Enemy, as there was in Eden, we do know that when Satan left Jesus in the desert following the three temptations, we are told in Luke 4:13, "When the devil had finished all this tempting, he left him until an opportune time" (NIV). Throughout the Gospels, we see no other circumstance where Jesus, aside from His rebuking Peter's defense of His death, was in a condition quite like this: "deeply troubled and distressed" and "crushed with grief."

Might this have been that predicted time from Luke 4, where the Enemy was hitting the Lord hard with everything he could to try to stop His sacrifice on the cross? If there was no temptation, then why was there so much struggle and grief? In the epic film *The Passion of the Christ*, Mel Gibson chose to depict the Enemy present with Christ in the garden. The intense level of Christ's battle in the Garden of Gethsemane makes total sense to consider the reality of the Enemy's presence.

Considering our look at Adam yesterday and now applying all we know of God in Scripture and what we know of Jesus' calling and mission, we can safely say that God intended for Jesus to:

- Protect his bride (the church, the body of Christ, about to be established)
- Purge the Enemy
- Pursue God's glory

And Jesus did all that and exactly that.

What made the difference? Well, let's bring back the final statement of Mark 14:36 that is left out above. Christ's final sentence of complete surrender was the game changer.

> *"Yet I want your will to be done, not mine."*

Jesus ultimately won back all that was lost and taken away in the first garden. The Last Adam redeemed all that had been lost and taken away by the First Adam. Inspired by the Holy Spirit, the apostle Paul introduced this idea of the First Adam and Last Adam to connect the two men, bridging the Old and New Testaments, the final connecting piece between Genesis and Revelation.

The first man was named Adam, and the Scriptures tell us that he was a living person. But Jesus, who may be called the last Adam, is a life-giving spirit. We see that the one with a spiritual body did not come first. He came after the one who had a physical body. The first man was made from the dust of the earth, but the second man came from heaven. Everyone on earth has a body like the body of the one who was made from the dust of the earth. And everyone in heaven has a body like the body of the one who came from heaven. Just as we are like the one who was made out of earth, we will be like the one who came from heaven. (1 Corinthians 15:45–49 CEV)

While we are saved by God's love and grace once, today and every day we must make the choice of whether to live in the powerlessness of the First Adam or the power of the Last Adam, in the sin of the First Adam or the redemption and righteousness of the Last Adam. Our opportunities to sin do not change upon salvation. The same temptations and sin are still available. But our choices—our options—are totally changed by the presence of Christ in our lives, coupled with the power of the Holy Spirit.

Surrendering to our sanctification—the transformation of our lives into the image of Jesus—becomes a moment-by-moment opportunity.

What are some clear ways you have experienced your own transformation from the First Adam to the Last Adam?

_____

_____

_____

_____

_____

_____

In what ways are you being sanctified today in your current transformation?

_____

_____

_____

_____

_____

_____

_____

"Heavenly Father, thank You for Jesus, for salvation, for redemption, for restoration, for transformation. Thank You for the Gospel being alive in my life every day. In Jesus' name, amen."

MEMORY VERSE

JESUS LOOKED AT THEM INTENTLY AND SAID,
"HUMANLY SPEAKING, IT IS IMPOSSIBLE.
BUT NOT WITH GOD.
EVERYTHING IS POSSIBLE WITH GOD."
- MARK 10:27 -

LEADERS ARE CONSTANT LEARNERS
TO MAKE SURE THEY CAN STAY
CONSISTENT TEACHERS.

We
love Him
BECAUSE
HE
LOVED US
FIRST.
1 John 4:19 NLV

CONGRATULATIONS ON COMPLETING 40 DAYS!

Everyone involved in the publishing of this book wants to encourage you to continue your new habit of spending time with God daily—reading His Word, praying, listening, journaling, applying what you hear, and growing in your faith. Your journey toward becoming a leader in God's legacy has begun!

While devotional books like this are great to use, we want to challenge and encourage you to arrive at the place where you sit down every day with God's Word to read, pray, listen, and obey. We have been given the greatest Book ever written, and God has something new to say to you every day by His Spirit.

Your Heavenly Father is inviting you to join Him in His work, so stand strong and be a leader for Him in all your circles of influence.

I pray that from his glorious, unlimited resources he will empower you with inner strength through his Spirit. Then Christ will make his home in your hearts as you trust in him. Your roots will grow down into God's love and keep you strong. And may you have the power to understand, as all God's people should, how wide, how long, how high, and how deep his love is. May you experience the love of Christ, though it is too great to understand fully. Then you will be made complete with all the fullness of life and power that comes from God. Now all glory to God, who is able, through his mighty power at work within us, to accomplish infinitely more than we might ask or think. Glory to him in the church and in Christ Jesus through all generations forever and ever! Amen. (Ephesians 3:16–21)

BEGINNING A RELATIONSHIP WITH GOD THROUGH JESUS CHRIST

If at any point as you went through this devotional, you had the question, "So how do I begin a relationship with God?" then first and most important, if at all possible, we recommend you talk to a pastor, priest, or mature Christ-follower regarding this significant spiritual decision.

Here is a simple explanation of the Gospel of Jesus Christ.

There is a God-shaped hole, or an emptiness, inside each of us. We all try to fill this void in our own way. We cannot see on our own that God Himself is the answer to our emptiness. His Spirit has to help us.

The Bible defines sin as attitudes, thoughts, and actions that displease God. Every person since Adam and Eve has had this problem. Even if we try really hard to be "good," we still make selfish decisions that are not pleasing to a perfect God.

In Paul's letter to the Roman church, he created a pattern that lays out a path to salvation in Christ. For millions of people, these simple yet profound truths have led to new life.

For ever since the world was created, people have seen the earth and sky. Through everything God made, they can clearly see his invisible qualities—his eternal power and divine nature. So they have no excuse for not knowing God. Yes, they knew God, but they wouldn't worship him as God or even give him thanks. And they began to think up foolish ideas of what God was like. As a result, their minds became dark and confused. (Romans 1:20–21)

We are made right with God by placing our faith in Jesus Christ. And this is true for everyone who believes, no matter who we are. For everyone has sinned; we all fall short of God's glorious standard. Yet God, in his grace, freely makes us right in his sight. He did this through Christ Jesus when he freed us from the penalty for our sins. (Romans 3:22–24)

But God showed his great love for us by sending Christ to die for us while we were still sinners. (Romans 5:8)

For the wages of sin is death, but the free gift of God is eternal life through Christ Jesus our Lord. (Romans 6:23)

If you declare that Jesus is Lord and believe in your heart that God raised him from the dead, you will be saved. For it is by believing in your heart that you are made right with God, and it is by openly declaring your faith that you are saved. (Romans 10:9–10)

For "Everyone who calls on the name of the Lord will be saved." (Romans 10:13)

For everything comes from him and exists by his power and is intended for his glory. All glory to him forever! Amen. (Romans 11:36)

Countless people have begun a relationship with God through Jesus Christ after reading Paul's words guiding to salvation. This is the truth of the Gospel. But God gives you the choice. If you are ready to begin a relationship with Christ, there is a strong likelihood that there is someone in your life who would love to know, and is ready to talk with you about this important choice and answer any questions to guide you in your decision. Please talk to someone as soon as you can.

If you know that you are ready to begin a relationship with Christ right now, while there are no magic words or specific formula for receiving God's gift of salvation, we have included a simple prayer for guidance:

"Dear God, I know I am a sinner and need Your forgiveness. I now turn from my sins and ask You into my life to be my Savior and Lord. I choose to follow You, Jesus. Please forgive my sins and give me Your gift of eternal life. Thank You for dying for me, saving me, and changing my life. In Jesus' name, amen."

For I am not ashamed of this Good News about Christ. It is the power of God at work, saving everyone who believes—the Jew first and also the Gentile. (Romans 1:16)

ACCOUNTABILITY QUESTIONS

Depending on the needs of your group, some of these questions you may want to answer every week, while others you may decide to switch up. Feel free to use what you like. You can also use these as a guide to write your own questions to fit your group.

OFFENSE:

- How was your relationship with God this week?

- How was your Bible reading/study this week?

- How was your prayer life?

- Did you pray with your wife/family?

- How did you grow in your marriage this week?

- How did you grow as a father this week?

- What is one teaching point you gained and grew from this past week?

- Where was your strongest place of spiritual growth this week?

- Is there a situation where you gave sacrificially?

- How did you see God use you this week?

- What was your greatest blessing this week?

DEFENSE:

- Was there a moment this week where you disappointed yourself?
- Has any particular temptation or sin been strong in your life this week?
- How have you done in your mind/thoughts this week?
- Have you struggled with a sexual temptation this week? How have you fought it?
- Have you committed any sexual sin?
- How has your attitude been this week?
- How has your mouth/speech been this week?
- Did you compromise your integrity this week?
- Was there a situation where you hurt or offended someone?
- Was there a situation where you were a taker without regard for the other person?

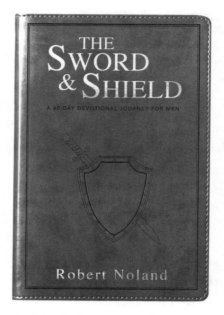